CHE GUEVARA

IN SEARCH OF REVOLUTION

CHE GUEVARA

IN SEARCH OF REVOLUTION

Calvin Craig Miller

MORGAN REYNOLDS

PUBLISHING

Greensboro, North Carolina

WORLD LEADERS

GEORGE C. MARSHALL
ADOLF HITLER
WOODROW WILSON
VACLAV HAVEL
GENGHIS KHAN
JOSEPH STALIN
CHE GUEVARA

CHE GUEVARA: IN SEARCH OF REVOLUTION

Copyright © 2006 by Calvin Craig Miller

Library of Congress Cataloging-in-Publication Data

Miller, Calvin Craig, 1954-
   Che Guevara : in search of revolution / Calvin Craig Miller.
      p. cm.
   Includes bibliographical references and index.
   ISBN-13: 978-1-931798-93-8 (library binding)
   ISBN-10: 1-931798-93-1 (library binding)
   1. Guevara, Ernesto, 1928-1967—Juvenile literature. 2. Cuba—
History—1959—Juvenile literature. 3. Latin America—History—
1948-1980—Juvenile literature. 4. Guerrillas—Latin America—
Biography—Juvenile literature. I. Title.
   F2849.22.G85M55 2006
   980.03'5092—dc22

                                    2006005975

Printed in the United States of America
First Edition

CONTENTS

Ernesto "Che" Guevara.
(Courtesy of Getty Images.)

ONE

Boy Soldier

Che Guevara died the same way many rebel fighters die. It was 1967 and the already mythical figure from the Cuban Revolution was leading a small band of guerrilla soldiers attempting to overthrow the government of Bolivia. Che hoped that the toppling of the Bolivian government would lead to a revolution in his homeland of Argentina. In early October Che and his men found themselves trapped at the bottom of the Churo Gorge. When they tried to fight their way out against Bolivian army troops trained by the United States, Che's greatest enemy, fifteen guerrillas died. Che, dressed in a threadbare and tattered uniform, was taken alive.

Che's captors took him to a schoolhouse in nearby La Higuera. The order of execution came the next day, October 9, 1967, and he was shot dead as he lay on a floor

The last known photograph of Che alive, October 1967. (AP Photo)

stained by the gore of previous executions. He was thirty-nine years old.

After Che's execution, Bolivian officers flew his body by helicopter to the small village of Vallegrande, where it was put on public display before being thrown into a mass grave filled with his fallen comrades.

In Cuba, Prime Minister Fidel Castro announced the news of Che's death on October 15. Castro praised the accomplishments of the man who had been his second-in-command during the struggle that brought him to power in 1959. The Cuban leader declared October 8 the Day of the Heroic Guerrilla Fighter.

Castro openly criticized Che's methods as a guerrilla fighter. "For as long as we knew him his actions were marked by an extraordinary impetuosity," Castro said. "Often we had to take steps, in one way or another, to keep him alive." He could have also mentioned that the Bolivian expedition was Che's third failed revolution in four years. He had tried to lead rebellions in Argentina and the Congo before taking up the campaign that cost him his life.

By time of his death, however, legend often took precedence over facts. Che had been a brilliant leader in the Cuban Revolution, leading a small band of rebels against regular army troops in a series of successful ambushes, overpowering columns of soldiers that outnumbered them by the thousands. Che's appeal was not limited to his military skill, however. He was a charismatic man who could lead men and women into deadly conflicts and who left a lasting impression on those who had met him.

The myth of Che began immediately after his death. During his funeral wake, giant posters of his handsome face hung from buildings in Havana, showing him in his trademark black beret with gold star, full beard, unruly dark hair, and clear-eyed, determined gaze. Within days he had received the ultimate tribute to a departed legend—thousands of people, particularly in Latin America, refused to believe he was dead.

Che's charisma also obscured his flaws, both while he was alive and after his death. It created an image of Che that, particularly in the United States and other developed areas of the world, is often out of sync with the reality of his life. By the end of the twentieth century, Che Guevara had entered the pantheon of truly mythical figures. His image, his writings, and the memories of those who knew him, including his enemies and those responsible for his death, combined to make him the model for one of the century's archetypes—the dedicated, revolutionary guerrilla.

This man, who would one day blame most of the world's problems on the disparity of wealth and opportunity he saw all around him, was born into one of the richest families in Argentina. Ernesto Guevara Lynch and Celia de la Serna, Che's father and mother, met in Buenos Aires in 1927. His mother's family descended

Opposite: _A crowd in Cuba pays tribute to Che in front of a banner with a quote of his reading: CREATE TWO, THREE, MANY VIETNAMS._ (Courtesy of Time Life Pictures/Getty Images.)

from the Spanish nobility; his father's great-grandfather had been one of the richest men in South America. While the preceding generations had diminished the family's wealth by the time Che was born on May 14, 1928, there was still enough for him to someday inherit a comfortable stipend.

Celia, Che's mother, graduated from a prestigious Catholic school at the age of twenty. Soon after graduation she met her future husband. Although her family held high position in the social order, Celia had a rebellious streak. Young women were not expected to handle their own financial affairs, but Celia insisted on managing her bank account and signing her own checks. She wore slacks and drove a car, in defiance of social convention. She proudly broke the rules whenever she could, even mischievously driving her car down the Calle Florida, a pedestrian street where cars were forbidden.

Che's father, Ernesto, had studied architecture and engineering, but confided to friends that he did not care for the monotonous details of such work. "I would rather shoot myself than sit behind a desk," he told a friend. Before earning a diploma, he left college to start a yacht-building company. The company turned a profit, but soon another business idea captured Ernesto's imagination.

Many South Americans enjoyed drinking maté, a South American tea similar to green tea. During the 1920s, the drink soared in popularity, swelling the profits for cultivators. Ernesto toyed with the idea of farming the plant and began to eye a plantation in Misiones,

1,200 miles from Buenos Aires. Ernesto wanted to buy the plantation, but he had invested most of his money in the yacht building business. His girlfriend, Celia, had the money.

Against the wishes of her parents, who wanted Celia to wait until she was twenty-one, she and Ernesto were wed on November 10, 1927. Celia was supposed to wait another year before acquiring her inheritance, but she filed a suit in court to obtain it early. The court ruled on her behalf, and she and her new husband set out for their newly acquired plantation in Misiones.

There the newlyweds built a house on their five-hundred-acre spread and began exploring their new property. At first, life on the plantation seemed like an adventure. "There, nothing was familiar," Ernesto later wrote, "not its soil, its climate, its vegetation, nor its jungle full of wild animals, and even less its inhabitants."

Ernesto implemented a working standard at the plantation that his son would later champion as a model of social justice. Rather than pay workers with money, many plantations gave their workers bonds that could only be used to buy overpriced goods at company stores. Agricultural workers in Argentina often toiled their entire lives without escaping poverty; sometimes they were kept on the land by threats of violence. Ernesto paid his employees cash. In a time when other plantation owners were feared and hated, Ernesto enjoyed the respect of the workers.

Living in such an isolated area caused hardships for

the couple, particularly when Celia discovered she was pregnant. She wanted her baby to be born with the best medical assistance available. Celia and Ernesto traveled to Rosario, a city north of Buenos Aires, for the birth. They also concealed Celia's pregnancy from her parents because the baby had been conceived before they were married. After the birth of Ernesto Guevara de la Serna, who would later be nicknamed Che, they took him to Buenos Aires to visit to his grandparents. The family called the firstborn Ernestito, a term of endearment.

In early May of 1932, Celia took little Ernestito swimming at the Club Náutica San Isidro. A cold wind was sweeping across the water and Ernestito was stricken with a severe attack of asthma, a respiratory disorder that would plague him throughout his life. Celia never forgave herself for taking him swimming, although it is unlikely that the incident caused his asthma.

Treatment for asthma required dry air, but the Misiones plantation was in an especially damp, humid area. Celia and Ernesto returned to Buenos Aires, where doctors advised them to take trips to Córdoba, where the air was drier. They eventually decided to take up permanent residence there and settled in Alta Gracia, just outside of Córdoba. Ernesto and Celia had four more children while living in the city: their first daughter Celia, then Roberto, Ana María, and Juan Martín.

The family was always short of cash. Ernestito's medical treatment was expensive, and the maté plantation

Ernestito with his parents and siblings at the pool in the late 1930s. (AP Photo)

yielded little profit. Ernesto turned his attention back
to his yacht-building business, but problems developed
when one of the investors pulled out because of falling
sales. Then the shipyard burned and destroyed the last
of Ernesto's investment. His inheritance gone, Ernesto
sunk into a depression. Despite their financial catastro-
phes, the Guevara family did not live as though they
were poor. They continued to take vacations and invited
neighborhood children to eat at their table.

Ernestito received special attention because of his
asthma. His father would sleep sitting up so Ernestito
could lean on his chest. Celia encouraged her eldest son
to stay physically active to build up his stamina. She set
an example by swimming in the treacherous currents of

the Paraná River. Ernesto would later think that his son inherited his bravery from his mother.

Ernesto and Celia Guevara believed strongly in social equality, despite their privileged backgrounds. No one was turned away from their dinner table hungry, even when they had to eat smaller portions to accommodate guests. Ernestito learned that his family could be traced back to Spanish nobility, but what his parents did influenced him more than who their ancestors were.

Celia and Ernesto encouraged their son to question conventional beliefs about morality and politics. Their society was deeply Catholic, but the Guevaras rejected most of the church's teachings. They considered themselves atheists and did not attend Mass. Ernesto and Celia agreed to have their children baptized but insisted that their education be secular.

Ernesto's architectural studies finally came of some use in 1941 when he was hired to improve a golf course in Alta Gracia. Ernestito made friends with the course caddies, the working-class boys who carried clubs and found balls for the golfers. Ernestito played on pick-up soccer teams with teammates from the lower classes. "As a child, [Ernestito] was a natural leader," recalled Delores Moyano Martin, one of his childhood friends. "[Ernestito], then about seven or eight years old, was the leader of a gang of kids, golf-course caddies and the sons of peons who worked in the nearby hills. He would often challenge the children of the local gentility and sons of well-to-do families vacationing in Alta Gracia to a soccer match." Ernestito's teams usually took the prize and celebrated their victories by taunting their more affluent rivals.

Ernestito's physical strength fluctuated depending on his asthma attacks. Doctors provided the family with an oxygen-filled balloon to relieve the symptoms, but Ernestito wanted to battle the illness with his own strength. His father later recalled his son's furious struggles: "He did not want to depend on this treatment, and he tried to bear the attack as long as he could, but when he could no longer stand it and his face was turning purple from the choking, he would wriggle and point to his mouth to indicate that it was time. The oxygen would relieve him immediately."

When he felt well, Ernestito exercised to build up his strength against the asthma attacks. In addition to soccer, he played war games. In the late 1930s and early 1940s, political events weaved their way into the boys' games and they used scenarios from the ongoing wars in South America and Europe in their mock battles.

When Bolivia and Paraguay went to war in 1932 over control of a territory called the Chaco Boreal, Ernesto sided with Paraguay. Both countries were landlocked and wanted to control the River Paraguay, which ran to the Atlantic Ocean. Bolivia and Paraguay lost more than one hundred thousand soldiers in the fighting. When Paraguay won the war in 1935, it claimed more than three-fourths of the Chaco Boreal. Following his father's lead, young Ernestito thought of Paraguay's soldiers as the "good guys."

Despite the political turmoil so close to home, the Argentinians had a different war on their minds. This one was in far away Spain where, from 1936 to 1939, the country erupted in a brutal civil war that overshadowed even the war in Argentina's neighboring countries. The Spanish Civil War pitted the elected Republican government, which advocated land reform and more state control over the powerful Catholic Church, against the more conservative forces of General Francisco Franco, who led a revolt manned by a large section of the army against the elected government. Franco allied himself with the other anticommunist dictators in Europe, such as Benito Mussolini in Italy and Adolf Hitler in Germany, as part of a political movement called fascism that spread through Europe during the 1930s. Fascists advocated radical nationalism and dictatorships that imposed strict social regimentation and suppression of all dissent. Fascist leaders harkened back to a romantic nationalism and said that only a strong leader could speak for his people.

Franco, a physically small man, was a natural leader who quickly emerged at the forefront of Spain's fascist movement in 1934 when he put down a miners' strike. Franco wanted to restore the monarchy, which had fallen in 1931, and to destroy the new Republican government, which was trying to diminish the privileges traditionally enjoyed by Spain's wealthy and aristocratic classes. The new government declared there was to be a separation between the church and the state and promised to remain neutral in future European conflicts.

In July of 1936, General Franco, aided by Mussolini and Hitler, led a rebellion against the Republicans. His fascist forces won the war and seized power in 1939. Franco would rule Spain for the next forty years. Many in Europe and North and South America saw the Spanish Civil War as a prelude to the coming international war in Europe and Asia. How one felt about the conflict, which side one supported, became an indicator of one's political ideology. Those on the left, for the most part, supported the Republican government. Rightists supported Franco and the army.

Ernesto and Celia fiercely supported the Republicans. One of Ernestito's uncles wrote about the war for a Buenos Aires newspaper, and when the war began to go badly and Republican refugees began arriving in Alto Gracia, they received a warm reception from the Guevaras. Ernesto formed a support group for the refugees and Ernestito and his siblings became friends with their children.

The war fired Ernestito's imagination, not just because of the leftist politics embraced by his family, but because he found war to be fascinating. He studied maps of Spain to trace the fronts and to follow the battles. His war games became more sophisticated and dangerous. The children fought so furiously with their slingshots and rocks that the combatants came away limping. In his imagination Ernestito was a commander leading charges against the fascists.

To school officials, however, he was not an army

commander but a boy who had delayed his formal education too long. In 1937, his parents reluctantly gave in to the insistence of authorities and enrolled him in school.

He had already learned to read at an advanced level and he received some credit for his homeschooling. Even so, he entered second grade a year older than most of his classmates and endured the typical taunts suffered by a new student. When fellow students mistook his asthma as a frailty, Ernestito was quick to show them differently. He even went out for rugby, a violent sport, where he took his share of blows and kicks and dealt them out as well. At times, though, his asthma betrayed him and he had to gasp at his inhaler.

The other students soon came to accept him. Argentina's public school system, unlike many in South America, took in pupils from all classes. Ernestito intermingled with both poor and affluent children, but held a distinct preference for his less prosperous playmates.

Ernestito always wanted to be a leader on the ball field. He soon developed a strong torso and biceps. Pictures taken of him around this time show a young man gazing at the camera with the physical pride he would keep his entire life. He had dark hair, high cheekbones, and brown eyes with a penetrating gaze. He seemed to enjoy having his photograph taken, putting on a solemn expression in one frame, flashing a mischievous smile in the next. He enjoyed being the center of attention and would shout for others to look out for him on the rugby field. He was also quick to take a dare. Once, when a schoolmate warned him to be careful with chalk and ink because they were poisonous, he bit off a chunk of chalk and washed it down with a drink of ink. He would walk on the top of a high narrow fence, like an acrobat, with cane stubs on both sides so sharp that a fall could be fatal. He took high dives into raging rivers and rode his bike down the middle of railroad tracks. Some said that Ernestito was not only "furibundo," furious, but also "el loco," a crazy person.

Ernestito's acts of bravado might have been attempts to compensate for his asthma. His parents tried everything within their power to cure him. On hearing of a folk remedy that called for the asthmatic to sleep with a live cat, Ernesto procured one and put it in the boy's bed. The unfortunate animal suffocated to death under the sleeping Ernestito. Because cold water seemed to bring on his attacks, Ernestito developed a lifelong aversion to bathing, which prepared him for life as a rebel.

The fluctuations in his physical health caused Ernestito to develop two sides to his character. When feeling well, he was a gregarious and outgoing leader on the rugby field, a furious and crazy daredevil who could deal out and take the hardest hits. Other times he was an introvert who preferred books over people. He devoured books written by everyone from psychoanalyst Sigmund Freud to science-fiction writers Jules Verne and H. G. Wells.

Ernestito also read, for the first time, the works of two nineteenth-century social writers and the founders of communism, Karl Marx and Friedrich Engels. The two

The program described in the Communist Manifesto *is termed* socialism. *The policies advocated for the abolition of land ownership and the right to inheritance, a progressive income tax, universal education, and the nationalization of the means of production and transport. These policies, which were to be implemented by a revolutionary government, would, according to Marx and Engels, be the precursor to the stateless and classless society known as* communism. (Library of Congress)

men collaborated on their most famous work, *The Communist Manifesto*, which was published in 1848 and called for the workers of the world to rise up in rebellion against what they called the bourgeoisie, the newly powerful middle-class owners of factories, land, and wealth being created by the industrial revolution. Marx and Engels called for the abolition of private property. Land should be owned by everyone and factories should be owned and operated by the workers, they argued, not by private individuals who had been able to amass great wealth while the majority struggled in poverty.

In Marx and Engels's ideal society, the state would control and manage the land and factories, deciding what food should be grown and what products would be produced, as well as who should receive what. Everyone should work to the best of his or her ability and receive what was needed. No one would accumulate property for its own sake.

Marx and Engels lashed out at the capitalist economies of Western Europe and the United States in their writings. In a capitalist, or free-market, system, private property is one of the highest values. Anyone with the means can own as much as they can accumulate, while prices and production are driven by supply and demand. Marx and Engels argued that capitalism inevitably exploited working people—many had to be poor so a few could be fantastically wealthy. Their idea of the perfect society was one without classes and where everyone worked together for the common good.

It is hard to determine how big an impression Marx, Engels, and other Communist writers had on Ernestito during his early youth. He did not talk or write much about the topic until he was a man. But it seems that the Guevara household tolerated and even espoused some Communist ideals. Celia and Ernesto were successful at passing on their political passions to their children.

During Ernestito's teen years, political uprisings and wars formed the backdrop to his education. Soon after the Spanish Civil War ended, Hitler launched his blitzkrieg attack on Poland and set off World War II. Germany's ally, Japan, drew the United States into the war in December 1941, when it made a surprise attack on a U.S. Naval base in Pearl Harbor, Hawaii.

Ernesto despised the Nazis, as he did all fascists. He told his children that if Hitler succeeded in taking over Europe, he would make Argentina one of his first targets when he turned his attention to the Western Hemisphere. In some ways Ernesto was fighting public opinion. Many Argentinians sympathized with the Nazis; after the war the country even became a haven for many former high-ranking German military and Nazi party officials fleeing prosecution in Europe. Following his father's lead, Ernestito organized a band of boys who supported the Allies, including the United States and Great Britain, in the war to stop Nazism. The boys spied on German settlements near Alta Gracia.

Argentina's government drifted in its position toward the Nazis, mainly because a series of weak presidents were toppled in quick succession between 1936 and 1943. One administration would oppose Germany and Japan, but the next would support them. In February of 1944, Colonel Juan Perón led a successful military coup against President Pedro Ramírez. Perón initially appealed to the Guevara family. He promised better conditions for workers and vowed to oppose fascism. He deported known Nazis and took over German companies. But Perón ruled as a dictator and suppressed _La Prensa_, the influential Buenos Aires newspaper owned by a cousin of Ernesto's. The family soon became enemies of Perón.

Politics was not the only source of strong passions in the family. The children and even the neighbors often

Leftist military officer Juan Perón was president of Che's home country of Argentina from 1946 1955 and 1973-1974. He is featured on here on the cover of Time *in November 1944.* (Time Archive)

heard shouting matches between Celia and Ernesto, who had begun to have affairs with other women. They remained married (divorce was not legal in Catholic Argentina), but the romance of their youth was gone.

Although Ernesto strayed from Celia, he remained close to his children. He shot bricks in target practice with Ernestito and his brothers and encouraged them to take long hikes. "I initiated my children in the secrets and dangers of life at a very early age," he said later. "I had the firm conviction that they ought to be free . . ."

Ernesto's lessons took root in Ernestito, who came to believe freedom could best be gained through travel. He made up his mind to see the world.

TWO

THREADBARE TRAVELERS

Before he could see the world, Ernesto Guevara de La Serna had to decide how he would earn his living. Like many young men, he was not sure what he wanted to do. In 1946, at the age of eighteen, he took a job with the public works office in Córdoba. Now he was no longer Ernestito, the darling of his parents, but Ernesto, a grown man. His plans were to work for a while before studying engineering at a university.

The Guevara family life had become more turbulent. Celia had run out of patience with her husband's affairs. A visitor to their home reported seeing Celia and Ernesto Sr. at their dinner table with two guns between them. Ernesto eventually left the house and rented an apartment.

The financial situation also worsened. Trying to administer the farm from 1,200 miles away was nearly impossible, and profits dropped as unpaid taxes mounted until Ernesto Sr. was forced to sell the property. The family moved back to Buenos Aires. Although they never descended into poverty, their lifestyle was greatly diminished. They drove around the city in a battered Plymouth.

Young Ernesto knew he would have to make his own way. He surprised his friends by switching his plans from engineering to medicine. He later said that he became interested in medicine partly because a doctor needed only his education and his instruments to get a job anywhere in the world. Of course, doctors had played an important role in his life. Another family health crisis may also have influenced his decision. In 1946, doctors diagnosed Celia with breast cancer and later performed a mastectomy. The same year, his ninety-six-year-old grandmother Ana suffered a stroke. Upon hearing of her condition, Ernesto quit his job and came home to be by her side. He helped take care of her during the last weeks of her life and was there when she died.

He applied to study medicine at the University of Buenos Aires. Soon after being accepted, he got a job as a research assistant with the famed allergist Dr. Salvadore Pisani, whom he had first met as a patient. The older man saw enough promise in Ernesto to give him a head start with his medical career.

Ernesto was a serious student, but he earned only average grades. He tended to work in spurts, cramming for tests after long periods of inattention. He had inherited his father's dislike of deskwork. While in class he longed to be outside on the open road. On weekends he would hitchhike or ride his bicycle throughout the countryside. He continued to play rugby roughly and enthusiastically, with his inhaler close by, and even launched a magazine devoted to the sport called *Tackle*.

Compared to his leftist parents, Ernesto was lukewarm on most political issues. However, it was during his university years that he began to delve deeper into the writings of Communist theorists. At first he considered their work to be more interesting as philosophy than as political doctrine. He read Karl Marx and Friedrich Engels with more interest than ever, and made a personal idol of Vladimir Lenin, who had led the Russian Communist Bolsheviks to power in 1917.

Born in 1870, Lenin had become a fervent opponent of the "czars," the absolute monarchs of Russia, as a young man. He joined the Russian Social-Democratic Worker's Party, which sought to overthrow the czars. Within the Social Democrats, however, there was great disagreement about how to accomplish this goal. Lenin argued the rebellion should be led by professional revolutionaries, while a rival faction wanted a larger, mass-based party more in line to what existed elsewhere in Europe. Lenin's party, the Bolsheviks, seized power in Russia in 1917 during the immense suffering caused by World War I.

After coming to power, Lenin and the Bolsheviks executed Czar Nicholas II and his family and renamed the country the Union of Soviet Socialist Republics (USSR).

Lenin and his successor, Joseph Stalin, attempted to transform Russia into a Communist state like that described by Karl Marx.

After Lenin's death, Stalin governed for nearly three decades. Stalin turned the Soviet Union into a nuclear and industrial superpower and took over adjacent countries. But in the process he condemned millions of his own people to death, either through violence or starvation. Later Communists would disavow Stalin as an

Bolshevik revolutionary Vladimir Lenin is mythologized during the 1917 revolution in Russia in this painting from the school of Soviet socialist realism. (Courtesy of Art Resource.)

aberration of the Communist ideal and refer to themselves as Marxist-Leninists. Ernesto admired Lenin because while he was a writer and theoretician like Marx, he was also a man of action.

Ernesto considered Argentinian president Juan Perón to be a despot who had come to power by military force and who had not fulfilled his promises for social reforms to help the poor and the workers. He did not want to serve in an army controlled by a man he despised. When he turned eighteen and had to register for the draft, he outwitted the army doctors by taking a cold shower just before he appeared for his physical. The cold water brought on a violent asthma attack, and his symptoms so alarmed the doctors they declared him unfit for service.

His dislike of showers became almost a phobia and his lack of hygiene was something of a campus legend. He would wear one shirt all week and then wash by wearing it during one of his infrequent baths. His classmates dubbed him "el Chancho"—the pig. Ernesto embraced the epithet by wearing dirty jackets and mismatched shoes and using a rope for a belt. He did not mind being mistaken for one of the poor citizens of Buenos Aires.

When it came to his dating life, Ernesto's good looks helped make up for his lack of hygiene. He frequented the tango dance clubs and even tried to learn to sing to impress the girls. But he had no musical ear and could not carry a tune. He did possess an ear for poetry, though, and would memorize it to impress girls.

Young Ernesto on the motorized bicycle he used to travel around South America during his travels in the early 1950s. (AP Photo)

In 1950, when he was twenty-two, Ernesto took the first of several journeys through the Americas. Eager for adventure, he decided finishing his degree could wait and made a crude motorcycle by strapping an engine to a bicycle. The first trip was to Rosario, his birthplace. Then he traveled to see Alberto Granado, a childhood friend who was working at a leprosy clinic in San Francisco del Chañar. Leprosy is a bacterial disease affecting the skin, nerves, and muscles, which causes sores and can lead to the loss of one's nose and fingers. Lepers were often shunned because of their disfigurement and because of fear of contracting the disease.

Alberto's compassion for these unfortunate patients made quite an impression on Ernesto, and he joined in the effort to ease their suffering. Alberto taught him how to diagnose and treat the disease. Ernesto saw that compassion was the most important trait for a physician. The two young men became attached to their patients.

Ernesto and Alberto planned another trip together, this time to the northern and western areas of Argentina, but mechanical difficulties thwarted their plans to travel together. Alberto abandoned the journey and Ernesto went on ahead. He had planned to travel into Chile, but turned back when the weather turned bad and the roads proved impassable.

Ernesto was invigorated by his travels and wanted to continue them. But first he had to resume his studies. Keeping up with his university work became more difficult in his fourth year at medical school, when he fell in love with Maria del Carmen Ferreyra, known by her nickname "Chichina."

The two met at a wedding in Córdoba. The daughter

of a wealthy family who appreciated the comforts wealth provided, Chichina seemed to symbolize the privilege Ernesto claimed to despise. But he was deeply in love. He asked her to marry him. Her family opposed him because she was only sixteen and because they did not think Ernesto, with his romantic visions of traveling the continent for a honeymoon and uncertain future plans, was a suitable match. Chichina was also unsure if she wanted to marry him. Ernesto was heartsick.

He decided that the best antidote for a broken heart was another road trip. Alberto reappeared in December of 1951 and suggested they take an extended journey to see the Andes Mountains, as well as Chile, Peru, Columbia, and Venezuela.

During this trip Ernesto kept a travel journal that was later published as *The Motorcycle Diaries*. The diaries reveal his developing social conscience as he witnessed the wrongs and injustices inflicted on the people of Latin America. They also reveal Ernesto and Alberto as cheerful vagabonds and bums who delighted in pranks and in freeloading. Occasionally, Ernesto comes across as cavalier about everything, including social conditions. But they also portray his gift for language and for clear, almost poetic, description.

The two set out on January 4, 1952, along with a young puppy dubbed with the English name "Comeback." They had little money and soon became expert hobos, successful at finding lodging in kitchens, barns, stables, or even in jail cells provided by local police.

Che's 1951 travels via motorcycle with Alberto Granado took him from his homebase of Alta Gracia, near Córdoba, Argentina, to many far-reaching parts of South America.

Sometimes they had to reluctantly pitch their tents. The biggest hassle was the frequent breakdown of their motorbike.

The trip was a liberating experience. Although he was nearly thirty, Alberto had never seen the ocean before they stopped at a beach early in their journey. For Ernesto, the ocean was an old friend, one whose wind "fills the senses with the power and mood of the sea."

They were grateful for the people who helped them along the way and were curious to learn about their lives and customs. When they had to, they worked for their board or for travel money, once doing chores for a ship captain who gave them free passage.

A few of the people who offered them generosity later regretted it. The husband of an Austrian couple who offered his barn as shelter warned them of pumas, jungle cats who were not afraid to attack people. His warning overheated Ernesto's imagination, and he thought he heard the snarl of the pumas in every night sound. When the family dog ran into the barn, Ernesto shot it with his revolver. He showed little remorse afterward, even after its owner threw her body over it, sobbing. The dog had been "nasty, ill-tempered," Che wrote, but they had to spend the next night in a field rather than ask for lodging in "a house where we were considered murderers."

In Barilouche, Ernesto received a letter from Chichina breaking off their relationship. He was at first so heart-broken he could not even write her a return letter. But he never mentioned her again in his diaries after his early pining for her. The majestic sights they encountered apparently worked as a curative for heartbreak.

The pair of travelers played a roguish trick on a newspaper in Chile that they were able to use to their advantage. When they passed themselves off as leprosy experts in Valdivia, a naïve reporter and editor took the bait and ran an article with the bold headline "Two Argentine Leprosy Experts Tour South America By Motorcycle." Motor travelers and homeowners who had seen the faces of the "experts" in the papers went out of their way to offer lodging, meals, and rides.

Near the town of Cullipulli, their motorcycle finally died. They got a ride to the town of Los Ángeles, Chile, where they left the bike in a fire station. After spending the night at the home of an army lieutenant, they had to cast aside the relative comfort of being "motorized bums" and resign themselves to the fate of "bums without wheels."

In Baquedano, on the road during a cold night, they met a Communist couple who had suffered for their political convictions. Over the light of a single flickering candle, the man told the young men of the persecutions he had faced by governments that considered all Communists to be dangerous. Free speech and political association were rarely protected in most of Latin America—simply being a Communist was a crime. The man had spent three months in jail and had been unable to find work after his release. His wife had nearly starved and had to leave their children with neighbors while seeking employment. The man darkly hinted that friends who shared his convictions had been killed by the police.

"The couple, numb with cold, huddling against each other in the desert night, were a living representation of the proletariat in any part of the world," Ernesto wrote. They did not even have a blanket, so he and Alberto gave up one of theirs. Although they nearly froze themselves, the incident "made me feel a little more brotherly toward this strange, for me at least, human species."

In Chuquicamata, the young men toured the copper mines. As they walked through the dismal corridors, they knew a debate was raging in Chile over who should own the mines. Some favored private ownership because the desire for profits would result in greater efficiency. The Socialists, Communists, and most left-wing groups wanted the mines to be "nationalized," or taken over by the state, so that the people would have some say over working conditions and profits. Ernesto was pretty clear on where he stood. "Whatever the outcome of the battle, one would do well not to forget the lessons taught by the graveyards of the mines, containing only a small share of the immense number of people devoured by cave-ins, silica and the hellish climate of the mountain," he wrote.

After leaving Chile, while on a bus to Caracas, Venezuela, weary of traveling, the two decided to split up. Alberto remained in Venezuela to look for a job. Ernesto traveled home by a circuitous route. He planned to take a plane to Miami, transporting horses owned by an uncle who bred them, and then return immediately to Buenos Aires.

This would be Ernesto's first encounter with the country he later denounced as the most monstrous on earth. Once his plane landed in Miami, its engine had to be repaired. The repairs took a month, giving Ernesto time to take a good look at a country his family had always criticized. Oddly, he did not write a word about Miami in his published diaries. No one, including the author, ever gave an adequate explanation why.

When Ernesto returned home that August, he was still full of youthful discontent, which had not yet found an outlet. That would come later in the jungles and valleys of Cuba.

THREE
YOUNG REBEL

Ernesto Guevara's journeys only whetted his appetite to travel. As he traveled throughout the Americas, he dreamed of journeying farther across the globe—to Europe, Africa, and all "the lands and seas of the world."

After returning to Buenos Aires, though, his urge to fight for social justice burned more intensely than his wanderlust. He had not traveled as a tourist. Instead, he had seen what he thought were the souls of the nations, which could only be found in "the sick of the hospitals, the detainees in the police stations or the anxious passengers one gets to know."

But before he could either travel or work for social change, Ernesto had to finish his medical education. His burgeoning idealism was wrapped up in becoming a doctor, and he still considered a doctor's training to be his ticket to travel because he could work anywhere in the world.

Fourteen exams stood between Ernesto and his medical degree. He threw himself into his studies, poring over his books for fourteen hours at a time, sometimes to the neglect of his health. Exhausted by his strenuous schedule, he failed to put the filter on a medical-waste-disposal machine, and the contaminated air made him so sick that he almost did not graduate. But he recovered in time to earn his degree in April of 1953.

Ernesto had no intention of setting up an office and practicing medicine in Buenos Aires. He considered his formal schooling as only part of the greater education he could get from life. His mother was dismayed when he told her of his plans for his next expedition. He and a friend, Carlos "Calica" Ferrer, planned to travel north to Bolivia and then to Venezuela, where his former traveling companion Alberto Granado was working in a leprosy clinic. Ernesto wanted to join Granado in his work. When they left the city, Celia wept and ran after the train.

On July 11, 1953, he and Calica arrived in La Paz, the largest city in Bolivia. They arrived on the heels of a revolution led the previous year by the Revolutionary Nationalist Movement, known in Spanish as the Movimiento Nacionalista Revolucionario (MNR). The movement had capitalized on the discontent created by the military government, which had led the country into economic stagnation and inflation. The MNR had nationalized the mines and turned over the once corporately owned land to poorer farmers. It had declared universal suffrage, dropping the requirements that voters had to own land or be able to read, thus increasing the electorate from 200,000 to a million voters.

The MNR's economic policies would eventually bankrupt Bolivia, but when Ernesto and Calica arrived, the MNR was still riding the wave of its recent success. The MNR's troops marched through the streets and erected billboards celebrating their cause.

In La Paz, Ernesto's lifestyle was similar to that of his youth. He sympathized with the poor but did most of his philosophizing about their plight at the dinner tables of the well-to-do. A family friend from Argentina introduced him in the high social circles of La Paz. Another friend suspected that Ernesto had an ulterior motive for seeking the friendship of the wealthy. He would eat for hours at a time, gorging himself at an unhurried pace. Like an animal in the wild, he was preparing himself for the long periods when he could find nothing to eat. When he left the fine homes, he returned to a dingy apartment where he hung his coat from a nail.

Ernesto and some friends decided to take the measure of the new government. They arranged to meet and interview the minister of peasant affairs. The day they arrived for the interview, Ernesto and his friends mingled with Quechua and Aymara Indians. Their faces and bodies were worn and dusty from the fields as they waited to apply for a government land-grant program.

At the entrance to the offices, a government official hosed the Indians down with a fine powder that turned out to be the deadly insecticide DDT to remove the lice and other vermin from their bodies.

Ernesto was shocked. "The [MNR] is carrying out the DDT revolution," he remarked. He put his objections ahead of good manners when introduced to the government minister. He demanded to know why the farmers were being put through such a dangerous ordeal. The minister claimed to share Ernesto's concern, but argued that the delousing was necessary because the native people had no understanding of hygiene and he could not let them infest the offices of the revolution. Ernesto wondered what kind of revolution would be so callous to the people they claimed to be helping. He predicted the MNR would eventually lose the people's support.

What troubled Ernesto more was Bolivia's continued reliance on the United States. During the 1950s, the Cold War tension between the United States and the Communist Soviet Union was the overriding concern of almost every diplomatic relationship the United States had with the states in Latin America and the rest of the world.

The Soviets and Americans had been allies during World War II. But it was an alliance of necessity that developed only after Hitler violated the nonaggression pact he had made with Joseph Stalin. Even during the war there was tension and jockeying for strategic position. The U.S. saw itself as the world's protector of the private enterprise system, while the USSR was committed to the theory of worldwide communism.

The end of World War II brought the former allies into conflict. Europe was divided by the occupying forces of the U.S. and Great Britain on one side and the Soviet Red Army on the other.

The war in Asia was ended by the U.S. dropping two atomic bombs on the Japanese cities of Hiroshima and Nagasaki. Four years after the American bombs ended the war with Japan, Russia developed its own bomb and soon the two sides were engaged in an atomic weapons race. Because nuclear war would probably result in total annihilation, a struggle to contain each side's influence developed that was given the name "Cold War" by Winston Churchill. Instead of a major "hot war," the conflict was carried out in a series of smaller "proxy" wars in Europe, Asia, the Middle East, Africa, and Latin America. The Cold War was also waged diplomatically and by clandestine intelligence agencies, such as the Central Intelligence Agency (CIA) for the U.S. and the Komitet Gosudarstvennoy Bezopasnosti (KGB) for the Soviets.

Latin America had long been considered by many U.S. policy makers to be the "backyard" of the United States, a vital area to protect from the influence of Communism by the use of both foreign aid and the threat of military intervention to limit Communist influence in the entire Western Hemisphere.

The demands of the Cold War led U.S. leaders to sometimes ignore the higher ideals of democracy and to form alliances with dictators committed to anticommunism. Some U.S. corporations, such the United Fruit Company, also had a powerful presence in the area, to the extent of sometimes controlling or corrupting governments and local officials in the search for cheap resources and labor. Examples of this apparent hypocrisy on the part of the U.S. infuriated many in Latin America. By the time he was an adult, Ernesto detested the influence the United States had in Latin America.

In Bolivia, Ernesto toured tin mines where the former government had ended miner strikes with machine guns. The MNR bragged that they had taken over the mines in the name of the people, but U.S. corporations were still the main buyer of Bolivian tin. Bolivia had nationalized the three largest mines, but now faced resistance from the Eisenhower administration, which was opposed to nationalization in principle. President Dwight Eisenhower warned the MNR against nationalizing more mines and against enacting land reform that would redistribute land to the peasants.

While the MNR struggled to implement reforms in Bolivia, rebels fighting the U.S.-backed Cuban government led by Fulgencio Batista were gaining momentum. Newspapers carried stories about a charismatic young Cuban revolutionary leader named Fidel Castro.

Cuban dictator Batista had been a force in Cuban politics for decades. As a young army sergeant, he led a successful revolt against dictator Gerardo Machado in 1933 and later forced provisional president Ramón Grau San Martín from power. He had been elected president

Cuban dictator Fulgencio Batista would become the target of Che's revolutionary fervor. (Library of Congress)

in 1940. He had started out as a popular figure; under his rule, Cuba adopted a progressive constitution that guaranteed basic freedoms and allowed for economic and political reform. Because communism appealed to many labor leaders, Batista had even legalized the Cuban Communist Party and included it in his governing coalition. The constitution prohibited him from running for a second consecutive term and, after leaving office in 1944, he moved to Daytona Beach, Florida.

Batista returned to Cuba in 1952 with hopes of regaining the presidency. He had to run in an election against two major political parties, the Auténticos and the Ortodoxos, the party to which Fidel Castro then belonged. But as election day neared, Batista found himself stuck in third place. Instead of accepting rejection by the voters, he decided to ignore their wishes. On March 10, 1952, he staged a coup and seized power.

Batista had underestimated the people's allegiance to their new constitution and the depth of their resentment at his trampling of voting rights. He further fueled their anger by presiding over one of the most corrupt governments in the Western hemisphere. The capital city of Havana became a haven of decadent Americans and other well-heeled tourists. Brothels and casinos operated openly, and Batista personally associated with leaders of the American Mafia, including such infamous gangsters as Lucky Luciano and Meyer Lansky. Political opponents were arrested on spurious charges and often tortured or killed.

Batista wisely maintained close ties with North American corporations, however. The U.S. government, although aware of the corruption, went along with Batista because he seemed to be a stabilizing force against the advance of communism in the region, although Batista continued to allow the Cuban Communist Party to operate without interference. The Communists maintained a truce by doing little to challenge Batista, even though they theoretically opposed his capitalist reforms. The

Cuban Communist Party seemed content to hold its meetings and publish newspapers praising the Soviet Union, all while being careful to avoid a confrontation with the government. Some party officials even accepted bribes from the Batista regime.

Other Batista foes were less complacent. Progressive intellectuals and students adamantly opposed Batista's unconstitutional seizure of power. Many more conservative Cubans were sickened by the corruption, prostitution, and gambling Batista permitted to thrive in Havana.

Fidel Castro had been a young lawyer running for election to the Cuban congress during the 1952 elections as a member of the Ortodoxos Party, when his political hopes were dashed by Batista's coup.

The next year Castro began to lead an armed revolt. On July 26, 1953, Castro and a small band of rebels attacked the Moncada military barracks in the southern city of Santiago. Batista's soldiers easily overpowered them and captured the revolution's leaders. Castro demonstrated defiance at his trial, denouncing the 1952 coup as well as the corruption and the atrocities he said Batista had carried out against his people. Castro turned the proceedings into a showcase for his political ideas, arguing that his revolution would bring fair distribution of land, more jobs, greater industrialization, and a better health and welfare system.

Castro succeeded in using the trial as propaganda for his ideas, but he was still convicted and sentenced to fifteen years in prison. When Batista, running unopposed,

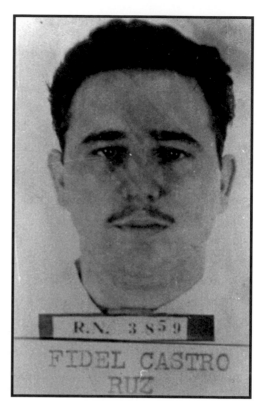

Fidel Castro during his imprisonment for the Moncada garrison attack in 1953. (Government of Cuba)

was elected to office the following year, he decided any danger presented by Castro and his little band of rebels was gone. He freed Castro along with a number of other political prisoners. This would prove to be the biggest mistake of his political career.

Meanwhile, Ernesto and Calica decided to continue their journey before they ran out of money. They obtained new passports and left Bolivia, traveling north through Peru and into Ecuador. In the coastal city of Guayaquil, they met up with friends they had made in La Paz. Ernesto grew close to one of them, Ricardo Rojo, who shared his opposition to the U.S. and his interest in radical politics. Rojo and three law students were on their way to Guatemala, where President Jacobo Arbenz Guzmán was trying to build a leftist government.

Rojo suggested that Ernesto and Calica join them in Guatemala. Ernesto jumped at the chance, but Calica was not as enthusiastic about the change in plans. He continued on to Venezuela, and Ernesto joined the group bound for Guatemala.

But first Ernesto had to make some money. He wrote and sold a couple of articles, his first success as a writer. One article criticized U.S. foreign policy, which he called imperialism; the other piece described a rafting trip on the Amazon River.

On their way north to Guatemala, Ernesto and his friends snuck a free ride on a ship owned by the United Fruit Company. Instead of being grateful, Ernesto developed an even deeper hatred of the company when he learned more about it. United Fruit was the most powerful American corporation operating in Central and South America. It monopolized railroads and ports from Guatemala to Cuba, bought up banana and sugar plantations, and imposed harsh working conditions. It was also involved in the politics of several nations and propped up corrupt dictators if they agreed to support its business activities. The actions of United Fruit even led the American press to coin the unflattering term "banana republics" to describe the countries in the region.

Ernesto called United Fruit an "octopus" because of its stranglehold on the economies of the countries where

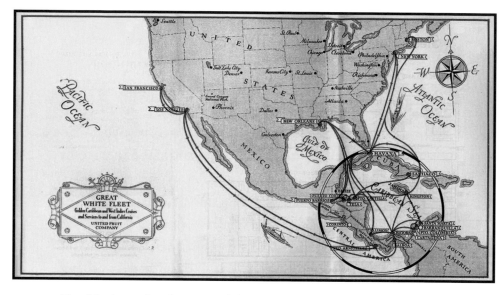

The shipping and cruise routes of the United Fruit Company's "Great White Fleet" connected both the west and east coasts of the United States to more than a dozen ports in Central and South America. (Library of Congress)

it operated. In a letter to his aunt, he wrote of his vow, "I would not rest until I see this capitalist octopus annihilated." He added another promise: "In Guatemala, I will improve myself and attain that which I need to become an authentic revolutionary."

In Costa Rica, on his way to Guatemala, Ernesto met some men who helped to change his life. They were Cuban revolutionaries, comrades of the now famous Castro and veterans of the 1953 Moncada barracks assault. They proudly called themselves "Moncadistas" and praised the courage of their leader. Their revolutionary spirit was contagious. It was not merely their ideas but their bold methods that thrilled Ernesto. He had been a leftist all his life, but had always seen social issues through the lens of philosophy. For the first time, he began to consider the possibility of forcing change through violence.

When he arrived in Guatemala in late 1953, Ernesto was at a crossroads. He was on the verge of transforming from an idealistic youth to an armed rebel. In Guatemala he met many people who shared his politics. Hilda Gadea was a Peruvian-born economist working for the new government. She was a short, stout woman that Ernesto did not find particularly attractive. In Peru, Hilda had served as youth leader of the People's Revolutionary American Alliance, an organization opposed to capitalism. She was bright, curious and devoted to her

Ernesto and Hilda, photographed on vacation at the Mayan ruins of Chichen Itza on Mexico's Yucatán penninsula. (AP Photo)

political beliefs. She and Ernesto read the same books and spent hours discussing the works of political authors and philosophers. Despite Ernesto's admitted lack of physical attraction for her, Hilda would eventually become his first wife.

He also spent time with Cuban rebels and their friends, several of whom were veterans of the Moncada barracks attack. They regaled him with war stories, some exaggerated, which fired his imagination. One of his best friends among the moncadistas was Antonio (Ñico) López, a lanky, six-foot-six twenty-one year old. Ñico told Ernesto about Castro's plan to build a new Cuba based on what was best for the workers.

His new Cuban comrades also gave Ernesto the nickname he would keep for the rest of his life. "Che" was originally a word of Italian origin, but in Argentina and other South American countries it had become a friendly way to hail a male stranger, somewhat similar to the North American expression "pal" or "buddy." Ernesto was proud of his new nickname. He had long opposed class distinctions and took satisfaction in having been dubbed with such a universal nickname. "For me 'Che' signifies what is most important, most loved in my life," he said later. "How could I not like it? Everything that went before, my name, my surname, are small things, personal, insignificant things."

The most significant thing, he thought, was the coming revolution. He was more convinced than ever that it was inevitable and would be unstoppable when it arrived. Like many young leftists from all over Latin America, he had traveled to Guatemala to personally witness the social experiment of President Jacobo Arbenz Guzmán, who had vowed to transform Guatemala through socialist reforms.

Socialism stands between capitalism and communism. Socialists believe that property and income should be under government control rather than the free market of capitalism, but also seek to build a less totalitarian government and to protect individual freedoms. Communists, on the contrary, argued that many of the individual freedoms celebrated in capitalist countries were illusions that served to distract from the reality that citizens were under the control of corporations and governments put in place to serve corporate interests.

President Arbenz, elected in 1951 with the largest majority vote in Guatemalan history, hoped to create national independence and economic stability through socialism without resorting to the total control Stalin had imposed in the Soviet Union and that was put in place in China after the Communists seized power there in the late 1940s. He attempted to steer a moderate course. He confiscated unused land owned by U.S. companies but agreed to pay them for it. He then turned the land over to landless peasants. Although he offered compensation, the companies complained they did not receive full value for their assets. Arbenz also aroused the suspicions of the Eisenhower administration by allowing members of the Communist Party to serve in his government. Because the U.S. was committed to keeping any hint of communism out of the Western Hemisphere, the Eisenhower administration began to discuss the possibility of intervening in Guatemala.

Arbenz's worst enemy was the United Fruit Company, one of the largest holders of unused land in Guatemala. United Fruit had enormous political influence in the United States. Secretary of State John Foster Dulles had once headed the law firm that represented United Fruit. When President Arbenz took control of 25,000 acres of United Fruit's land, the company complained bitterly to its friends in Washington.

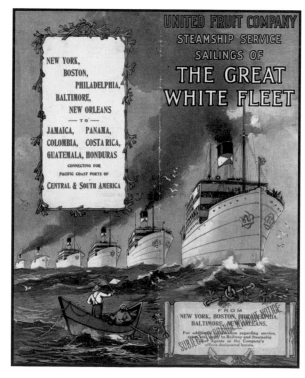

A promotional poster for United Fruit, the company whose policies in Central and South America provided Che's first glimpse of the need for socialist revolution in Latin America. (Library of Congress)

UNITED FRUIT COMPANY
STEAMSHIP SERVICE
SAILINGS OF
THE GREAT
WHITE FLEET

NEW YORK,
BOSTON,
PHILADELPHIA,
BALTIMORE,
NEW ORLEANS
— T O —
JAMAICA, PANAMA,
COLOMBIA, COSTA RICA,
GUATEMALA, HONDURAS
CONNECTING FOR
PACIFIC COAST PORTS OF
CENTRAL & SOUTH AMERICA

President Jacobo Arbenz of Guatemala was ousted in a 1954 coup organized by the CIA, and was replaced by Colonel Armas, who led the country for three rocky years before his assassination in 1957. After losing power in Guatemala, Arbenz fled to Cuba. He died in 1971 under suspicious circumstances in his bathtub in Mexico. (AP Photo)

Dulles, who, as secretary of state, was the president's top foreign-policy advisor, began to argue that Arbenz was actually a Communist who threatened the safety of the United States. Dulles' brother and former United Fruit executive Allen Dulles became director of the CIA in February of 1953. One of his first missions was to plan an invasion of Guatemala.

The Soviet Union supported anti-U.S. regimes around the world, but its support of Arbenz backfired. In May of 1954 the United States discovered a Soviet ship carrying weapons to Guatemala. This gave the state department and CIA evidence to justify an invasion. The

CIA organized "Operation Success" to overthrow Arbenz, and recruited the Guatemalan exile Colonel Carlos Castillo Armas to lead the campaign.

In June, Colonel Armas led a group of U.S.-supplied Guatemalan exiles into the country. As the band of 150 soldiers moved toward Zacapa, a small town in the east, Che prepared to defend the president. He told his family Arbenz would prevail against this small army of mercenaries and that he planned to offer his services as a soldier or doctor, wherever he was needed. This battle against a proxy army of the United States was just the anticapitalist fight Che wanted.

In support of the Armas coup, CIA planes bombed the capital for a week and also dropped propaganda leaflets. The bombing raids did little military damage but aroused fear in both the populace and the military. To Che's surprise, most army units simply refused to fight. When he and other volunteers showed up at a military base, the soldiers refused to issue them weapons. It was clear that his army would not fight to defend the government and Arbenz resigned on June 27.

Che was outraged that Arbenz had refused to fight, or to even accept his and others' offers to help. He wrote that "He [Arbenz] could have given arms to the people and he did not want to, and this is the result." It was a lesson Che never forgot. He decided that when a country was taken over by a revolutionary army, the first thing they should do was dismantle the regular army. When Arbenz had asked the regular army for help they deserted him, some out of cowardice but many others because they were not loyal to the president's socialist ideals. Arbenz's defeat by such a small band of soldiers was the final step in Che's transformation into a full-fledged, militant revolutionary. "I was born in Argentina, I fought in Cuba, and I began to be a revolutionary in Guatemala," he later wrote.

After Arbenz's collapse, however, Che's immediate goal was to stay alive and out of jail as Armas began a crackdown on Arbenz's supporters. When Hilda was arrested, Che sought refuge in the Argentine embassy.

Armas gradually began to ease up on the crackdown. He issued visas to those such as Che who had taken refuge in embassies and released some of the prisoners, including Hilda. She and Che discussed what their next move should be and decided to go to Mexico City, the new gathering place for radical leftists. Hilda first wanted to make a visit to her home country of Peru, so Che traveled ahead to Mexico, eager to find a conflict that could use his services.

FOUR
GUERRILLAS IN TRAINING

When Ernesto "Che" Guevara arrived in Mexico City in June of 1954, he was sure a major armed revolt against the capitalist countries would begin soon and that it was his destiny to be a leader of this rebellion. In the meantime, however, he needed to find work.

Che bought a cheap camera and became a street photographer, taking shots of tourists and selling them the prints. His best customers were those without cameras, but most tourists traveled with cameras. "The potential market is enormous, but the real market, make no bones about it, means slow starvation," he joked to his old friend, Ricardo Rojo.

He also sold books, giving him a cheap way to feed his appetite for reading, and did volunteer work at a hospital, although he made no serious attempt to set up a medical practice. He knew by now he wanted to use his medical skills in the service of an armed rebellion. He would become a battlefield medic, if needed, but he wanted first to be a soldier.

Hilda Gadea soon joined him in a small apartment on Nápoles Street. Their relationship continued much as it had in Guatemala, both ambivalent about their level of commitment. In later years, each would insist the other had wanted to get married.

Che reunited with his rebel friends from Guatemala while volunteering at the general hospital when Ñico López, the lanky moncadista who had told him so many tales of Castro's revolt, came in to help a friend seek treatment for his allergies. Ñico and Che rekindled their friendship, and, through Ñico, Che met the Cuban rebel leaders, who were hoping Batista would soon let Castro out of prison.

Batista's victory in the 1954 election had inflated his confidence, although his only opponent had withdrawn before the vote. Batista apparently confused the fact he could intimidate anyone from running against him with actual public support. Before the election, he had declared a ninety-day state of siege and suspended civil liberties. After the election he lifted the order, and business boomed, particularly the tourist trade. Wanting to put a more benign face on his regime, he began releasing political prisoners. In May of 1955, he released eighteen former rebels, including Fidel Castro and his brother Raúl.

Castro was released without being forced to recant his revolutionary views. He almost immediately called for the formation of the "July 26 Movement," named after the date of the Moncada barracks assault, with the goal of overthrowing Batista. But the Castro brothers knew they had to temporarily leave Cuba. They decided to set up training camps in Mexico to prepare for another assault on Batista's regime. Batista's secret police learned of their plans, and Raúl barely escaped arrest before he got out of the country.

Che's Cuban friends introduced him to Raúl Castro in June of 1955. Raúl thought that the well-educated, passionate Che would be a valuable recruit. Che shared the Castro brothers belief in the use of force to bring about socialism. Raúl promised to introduce Che to Fidel as soon as his brother arrived in Mexico.

In the meantime, Che made a new friend that would mark him as a suspicious character in the eyes of United States officials. Raúl introduced him to Nikolai Leonov, who worked at the Soviet foreign ministry. The political ties between Raúl Castro and Leonov were not deep; they had met at a European youth festival a few years earlier. Che impressed the Russian with his intense curiosity about Russian politics, and Leonov lent him some books. Che joined the Russian-Mexican Cultural Relationships Institute, a group that brought together Mexican Marxists with Russian officials. The American CIA kept close tabs on the Soviet Embassy in Mexico City, as well as anyone else in the city openly professing Communist views. Before long the name "Che Guevara" began to appear in CIA files.

When Fidel Castro arrived in Mexico City in July 1955, he wanted to be careful not to take any action that would attract attention from the United States. His confinement in Batista's prison had strengthened his animosity toward the Cuban regime, but to get swept up in the Cold War tensions between the United States and Soviet Union at that stage could destroy his movement before it even began. Later, when he traveled to the United States to raise money, he presented himself as a nationalist leader, not as a Communist. He had seen what happened to Arbenz, who had merely advocated democratic socialism.

Castro led a small group of about eighty revolutionaries while in exile in Mexico. Known as the July 26 Movement, the small band plotted strategy for the best way to overthrow Batista.

Raúl followed through on his promise to introduce Che to his brother. Fidel and Che hit it off and talked all night their first meeting. Castro was a tall, muscular man who sported a dapper mustache. (He would later grow the full beard that came to symbolize his image and that of most of the rebel fighters.) He was a charismatic and energetic man of great stamina who could talk for hours at a time, with a knack for converting the skeptical to his way of thinking. Che needed little persuading to join his effort. Castro's plans for a new, socialist Cuba matched Che's aspirations, as did the idea of fighting a guerrilla

Fidel Castro (left) and Che in 1953, in the early days in Mexico City, during which Castro's small group of revolutionaries spent day and night discussing and planning their next move. (AP Photo)

war in the jungles of Cuba. When Castro offered him the position of doctor to his small band of guerrillas, Che accepted.

Che had met many people who talked of leftist causes with great enthusiasm, but he knew Castro was not just a talker. He knew Castro would "stop whining and fight."

On the heels of his joining Castro's rebels, Che became a father. Hilda informed him that she was pregnant not long after his first meeting with Castro. They married in August, and she bore a girl they named Hilda Beatriz in February of 1956. Che doted on little "Hildita." Outwardly, he was a joyful husband and father, taking hikes, exploring ruins, and quoting poetry with his bride. In his journal, however, he confessed doubts that the marriage would last. He was already more devoted to Castro and the revolution than to his new family.

Castro and Che came from similar backgrounds, although Castro had no noble ancestry. Ironically, Castro's father was the sort of self-made man American capitalists admired. Born a peasant, he amassed holdings in sugar, timber, and land. Castro went to a Catholic school, where he became known for getting into fights and questioning authority. He enrolled at the University of Havana Law School in 1945 but spent as much time on political activity as he did on his studies.

In 1948, Castro attended a student conference in Bogatá, Columbia, called to protest United States involvement in South America. During the conference, Jorge Eliezer Gaitán, leader of the Colombian Liberal Party, was assassinated. It was suspected that the Colombian government was behind the assassination. Popular with students, Gaitán had advocated change through democratic means. Castro came to think that Gaitán's democratic idealism had gotten him killed. However, at the time he was still unwilling to give up on the democratic process. He decided to run for a seat in Cuba's House of Representatives in 1952, but the election was thwarted by Batista's coup.

Castro renounced the electoral process. Che had also become cynical about democracy, particularly after Arbenz's failure in Guatemala. Arbenz had won a landslide popular victory but was easily displaced by skilled fighters. His political popularity had not protected him from the CIA and armed counterrevolutionaries. Furthermore, Che thought that Arbenz had allowed his enemies to criticize him too much and that they should not have been allowed to operate openly. Democracy, Che and Castro decided, was an illusion promoted by the U.S. and other capitalist powers to make it easier to stamp out incipient Marxist revolutions. It was best to seize power and do what was necessary to install a strong, Marxist government. To attempt to maintain democratic ideals, such as free speech and free assembly, served only to undermine the revolution.

Castro knew he had to sell his image carefully to American journalists, most of whom believed in democracy. This meant hiding his actual ideas about the government he wanted to install in Cuba. He had gained world press attention with his daring attack on the Moncada barracks. Many in the press disliked Batista's dictatorial tactics and were looking for an attractive alternative. Newspaper reporters sought out the charismatic Castro.

Castro's efforts were helped by what was going on in Cuba in the 1950s. Greed fueled governmental corruption, with many high-ranking officials sharing in the bounty of illegal payoffs and bribes and companies seeking contracts for public projects such as highways and railroads making payoffs to Batista and his cronies. Batista even took a percentage of the profits from the lucrative casino businesses operated by the American

Mafia, who considered this the cost of doing business in Cuba.

For most ordinary Cubans, Batista's reign brought misery. Peasants farming the countryside could not afford to buy their own land, and workers struggled to find jobs in the cities. While the overall economy boomed during the 1950s, due primarily to high demand for sugar, few benefited. Batista made little effort to implement programs for the public good.

Batista terrorized the political opposition. His enemies would suddenly disappear. His rule angered university professors and other intellectuals who wanted democracy restored. The University of Havana became fertile ground for those who wanted to see the dictator overthrown. In late 1955 students staged anti-Batista riots and demonstrations. Batista's police beat the protesters and, in some cases, killed their leaders. Police interrogators frequently used torture as a means of extracting information and spreading fear.

Batista maintained ties to the U.S. by denouncing international communism. Meanwhile, Castro kept his Marxist views secret. In interviews he painted himself as a man of the people.

Che introduced his friend Ricardo Rojo to Castro. Castro was cooking a big pot of spaghetti in the kitchen of his apartment and amiably explaining his ideas and strategy the first time Rojo met him.

After raising sufficient funds, Che and the other rebels began training with guns. Colonel Alberto Bayo trained the guerrilla forces. Bayo, a one-eyed veteran of the Spanish Civil War, set up camp at a ranch twenty-five miles outside Mexico City. The compound was imposing, with a six-hundred-square-foot house surrounded by nine-foot stone walls and observation towers. Castro appointed Che chief of personnel and he served as Bayo's second in command.

The guerrillas arose every morning at five and trained until dark. Bayo taught them the use of camouflage, ambush, counterattack, and defense tactics to be used against planes and tanks. They took long marches without food and water, deprivations they would endure soon enough in combat. Bayo set up rival camps on an opposite mountain range, so the soldiers could stage mock ambushes for their war games.

The regimen demanded more than most recruits could give at first. One particularly tough round of exercises left almost all of them panting on the ground. But Fidel and Che insisted that the day was not over. They still had to calibrate their rifles. Most of the soldiers were physically unable to follow his orders and Fidel upbraided them. Why were they unable to push themselves any further when this Argentinian, who had never set foot in Cuba, still had the strength to carry on?

Bayo had the daunting task of teaching Castro's men the essentials of guerrilla warfare. In guerrilla war, as opposed to conventional combat, rebels avoid frontal confrontation with the superior forces of a regular army. When the enemy attacks, guerrillas give way, disappearing into the jungle. When the army takes ground, guerrillas take cover and wait. When the enemy soldiers grow complacent or weary, guerrillas attack, usually from the flank or rear. This kind of fighting seemed cowardly to many of the young men, and Castro had to convince them it was the only way Batista could be defeated. He reminded them that his assault on the Moncada barracks had been a frontal attack, and that he had paid for his recklessness with imprisonment.

Bayo struck up a close friendship with Che. The two played chess at night while Che relentlessly quizzed Bayo about guerrilla tactics. Bayo gave Che the highest marks of any man in camp. When asked to explain why Che got top honors, Bayo replied, "Because he is, without a doubt, the best of everybody."

Mexican police put Che's mettle to the test soon after his training ended. On June 20, 1956, six days after Che's twenty-eighth birthday, police raided the training camp. Batista's agents had bribed the police to monitor the rebels' activity, and they arrested the guerrillas, including Che.

Under interrogation, Che made no effort to hide his political affiliations, admitting that he was a Marxist-Leninist. Castro went into a fury when he heard of Che's admission. He had taken pains to keep everyone, particularly U.S. leaders and the American public, in the dark about his own political affiliations.

Behind bars, Castro used his connections with sympathizers, including a police official, to obtain the release of most of the men. A combination of bribes and

Twenty-two Cuban exiles arrested for plotting the assassination of President Fulgencio Batista are shown in front of a government office in Mexico City June 26, 1956. Fidel Castro stands at center right, in sunglasses, next to the woman in the white dress. Che is seated second from left. (AP Photo)

influence got all but Che and one other rebel out. Che's admission of his Marxist-Leninist beliefs had lengthened his stay in jail, but he was eventually bribed out.

Castro was running low on funds and still had to buy a boat to sail his rebels into Cuba. He decided to strike a deal with an unlikely ally. Former Cuban President Carlos Prío Socarrás wanted Batista overthrown for his own reasons. He was a likely rival of Castro's after Batista fell. It is not quite clear why Prío Socarrás agreed to cooperate with Castro. Perhaps he hoped Castro's band of rebels would topple Batista, then be incapable of governing. Castro secretly traveled to Texas for a meeting with Prío Socarrás.

Whatever Prío Socarrás's reasoning, Castro walked out of his meeting with the former president $50,000 richer. He used the money to buy a boat and supplies. He paid $20,000 for the *Granma*, a pleasure yacht built to hold ten or twenty passengers. The vessel was in bad shape and needed repair, but Castro did not want to wait. Informers had warned Batista would attack them soon.

On November 23, Castro summoned the rebels to the small town of Poza Rica, near Tuxpán. They spent the next two days preparing the *Granma* for its passage, loading uniforms, rifles, and antitank guns on board and patching the old boat as much as possible.

On the night of November 25 a cold northern storm bore down on the Gulf Coast. Melba Hernández, one of Castro's underground supporters from the days of the Moncada assault, watched in disbelief as his soldiers

The Granma's *treacherous voyage from Poza Rica to Belic took approximately a week.*

prepared the rickety ship. She told him it could not possibly hold more than a dozen men. Castro summed up his resolve in a few words. "I wouldn't deceive you. About ninety are going," he said, then shook her hand. "It's time."

Che had sent his mother a letter before departure proclaiming his confidence but preparing her for his death. He believed guerrilla tactics could work against large armies. But Colonel Bayo's top pupil had only fought in war games. As the *Granma* sailed with lights out into the dark waters of the Straits of Florida, Che and eighty-one other soldiers prepared to test their mettle against the regular army of Batista.

FIVE
A DANGEROUS LANDING

As the *Granma* entered the Gulf of Mexico, several of the rebels soon turned pale and began to vomit. They had no seasickness medicine. Most of the eighty-three men, with the exception of a few seasoned sailors, had to ride out their symptoms. Che did not suffer from seasickness, but he did have asthma attacks. At one point they thought the ship had sprung a leak and threw their surplus supplies overboard, only to discover afterward that a faucet had been left running.

This pasty-faced crew did not look like formidable insurgents. After a few days at sea their seasickness settled down, but their landing in Cuba followed the helter-skelter pattern of the expedition. On December 2, 1956, the *Granma* ran aground in a swamp near a place called Belic.

A traditional military officer would have probably considered Castro's rebels to be on a suicide mission. They planned to overpower Batista's army of forty thousand with eighty-two soldiers. In the battles to come, casualties and desertions would sometimes reduce the number of ragtag troops to as few as eighteen. They picked up new recruits as the revolt continued, but they never numbered more than a few hundred. In addition to the army, Batista had an air force. A well-armed regiment guarded each of the country's provincial capitals.

Batista's soldiers soon launched an attack on the outnumbered rebels. A Cuban coast-guard cutter had spotted them soon after the *Granma*'s landing and alerted the armed forces. A helicopter circled low overhead the first morning, followed soon after by an air force attack. Fortunately, the swamp provided a ceiling cover that made the rebels hard to target from the air. But the water was so deep the soldiers waded up to their shoulders and had to leave much of their equipment behind. They slogged through the swamp for two hours before reaching a narrow strip of beach. "We reached solid ground, lost, stumbling along like so many shadows or ghosts marching in response to some obscure psychic impulse," Che later wrote.

In the early morning of December 5, they reached a place called Alegría de Pío, bordered on one side by a cane field and on the other by a valley leading to dense wood. That afternoon the planes bore down on them again. Men ran in all directions to escape the blasts ripping the earth.

Che was as desperate as any of them as he scrambled for cover. He fumbled his way through the supplies, finding two boxes, one filled with medicine, the other with bullets. He grabbed the bullets. Later, he would point to this split-second decision as the moment he became a soldier instead of a doctor.

The bombs and bullets turned the cane field into a gory scene. The wounded screamed and clung to sugar cane stalks in a futile attempt to find cover. A bullet ripped through Che's neck, and for a few moments he was lost in what he thought was the final reverie of his life. He remembered a story by Jack London called "To Light a Fire" about a freezing man in Alaska who, after failing to light a fire, leans against a tree and accepts his death with dignity. Che prepared to do the same, but fellow rebel Juan Almeida refused to acquiesce in Che's noble plan and urged him to his feet. The injury turned out to be a flesh wound and Che stopped the flow of blood with the pressure of his hand.

The guerrilla band struggled onward until it reached the forest of the Sierra Maestra chain. They were nearly starved, some of them having eaten grass or raw corn, others raw crabs. Only a handful survived the initial attack. Written accounts vary on the number of survivors, some saying fifteen, others twenty. Che recorded twelve. Among the dead was Ñico López, the lanky soldier who had regaled Che with stories of the Moncada

The Sierra Maestra, a coastal mountain range in southeast Cuba, is the highest system of mountains on the island. Pico Turquino is the range's highest point, at 6,560 feet. (AP Photo)

barracks raid and introduced him to the Cuban revolutionary movement.

As the guerrillas regrouped in the mountains, peasants, tired of Batista's dictatorship, joined their forces, helping replace the soldiers lost. Che wrote of the terrible suffering the rebels had endured for their cause, but nonetheless recalled his first days in Cuba fondly. "These were happy hours, during which I acquired a taste for my first cigars (which I learned to smoke as a way of driving away the overly-aggressive mosquitoes, until I was captured by the fragrance of the Cuban leaf), as projects for the future followed one another rapidly."

Batista wanted to capitalize on his troops' initial success. The government spread the rumor that Fidel and Raúl had been killed. Che was also listed among the dead, sending the Guevara family in Buenos Aires and Hilda Gadea in Mexico City into despair. Che's loved ones soon found out that the Cuban government was lying when the Argentine embassy sorted through the dead and did not find Che among them. Later Che smuggled out an airmail letter to his mother, assuring her he was alive and intending to fight on. He closed by

Fidel leads anti-Batista guerrillas in the wilds of the Sierra Maestra. (Courtesy of Getty Images.)

ironically urging her to "have faith that God is an Argentine."

The rebels did not spend all their time in forests. They held planning sessions for further battles in the houses of peasant sympathizers. The guerrillas wanted not only to attack the regular army but also to exact vengeance against plantation foremen, who were often thugs who ruled the plantations as harshly as Batista's police ruled the cities. If they could make an example of these men, the rebels thought, more peasants would come to their side.

On the night of January 16, forty four days after landing, the rebels crossed the La Plata River and took positions on the road leading to an army barracks. Soon a foreman rode by on a horse, drunk, and Fidel approached him pretending to be a colonel in Batista's army, asking for directions to the garrison.

What happened next took its place among the folklore of the revolution. The foreman amiably rambled in a slurred voice about how he would like to get his hands on this or that rebel, particularly Castro. Fidel agreed that this Castro man should be killed, and the foreman showed him boots he had taken from a dead rebel. He then led the disguised rebels to the barracks, pointing out where a sentry was stationed as well as the guard's sleeping quarters.

The man's antics sealed his fate. Castro revealed himself and had the man arrested and executed as soon as the attack started.

After they surrounded the soldiers quarters, Fidel fired the first rounds from his submachine gun. The other rebels opened fire on the barracks with pistols, rifles and machine guns. Castro then gave the order to cease fire and called for the soldiers inside to surrender. Batista's men answered with a round of bullets.

The rebels returned fire before struggling through a series of blunders. Che tossed a grenade that did not explode and another soldier threw a stick of dynamite that fizzled out. Then Che and another guerrilla ran across a clearing and set fire to a thatch-roofed hut. The regular soldiers, apparently more alarmed at the prospect of being burned out than shot, surrendered.

The rebels had killed two soldiers and wounded five and collected a store of supplies, including a Thompson submachine gun, eight Springfield rifles, a thousand rounds of ammunition, food, and clothing without losing a man.

Well-armed and at last well-fed, the rebels capitalized on their success two days later when they ambushed more army troops at a place Che christened Arroyo del Infierno (Hell's Creek.) Castro had begun marching by day, hoping to draw the enemy into pursuit. It took two days for the army to catch up with them, but when they did, they found themselves nearly surrounded by a semicircle of rebels.

Castro shot and killed one soldier before the other rebels opened up in a crossfire that trapped the army soldiers, killing five of them before the army retreated thirty minutes later.

Che killed his first man at Arroyo del Infierno, an act that changed him forever. He shot at the soldier from twenty yards away and missed with his first shot. When he fired again the man's rifle fell from his hand, and the bayonet stuck in the ground as he tumbled backwards into a house. Che ran into the house and examined the body. He had shot his foe in the heart, killing him instantly.

After the defeat, Batista once again sent his air force into the fray. On January 30, five American-made planes appeared in the skies over the guerrilla camp on Mount Caracas. The guerrillas watched as the best bomber and fighter planes from World War II bore down on them, raining bombs and bullets into their camp. Fortune smiled on them again, however. The rebels happened to be two hundred yards away from their main encampment when the attack started, and not a single guerrilla died in the attack. The air force tried twice more, on February 7 and February 8, without killing a single man.

The air raids did inflict psychological damage, however, and forced the rebels to keep on the move. It also left them with a question: How had the air force known where to target its attacks? They began to suspect there was a traitor in their midst. Che was determined to find the turncoat and execute him. On February 9, an infantry attack surprised the rebel fighters, scoring no casualties but redoubling suspicions.

There was a spy among them. A peasant named Eutimio Guerra had first served the rebels as a guide before

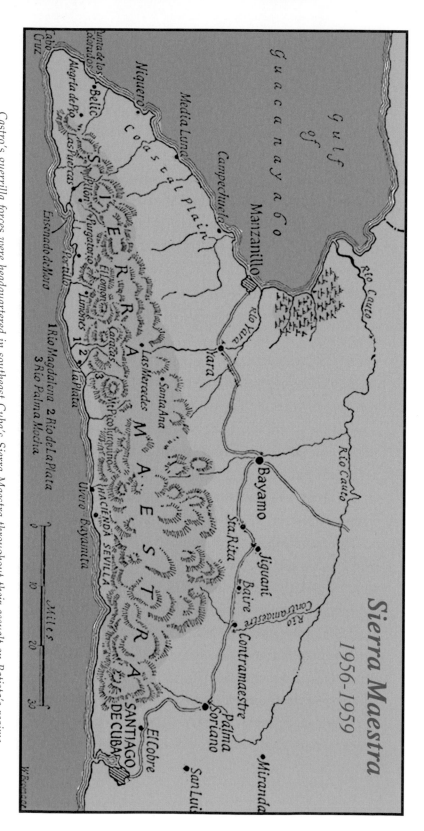

Castro's guerrilla forces were headquartered in southeast Cuba's Sierra Maestra throughout their assualt on Batista's regime.

being captured by Batista's men. Guerra had cracked under interrogation and the threat of torture and agreed to report on the movements of the guerrillas. When one of the rebels caught Guerra with a safe conduct pass from an army officer, the traitor fell to his knees and asked to be shot. He asked only that the revolution take care of his children.

The rebels were unsure of what to do. This was the first time they had uncovered a traitor in their midst. Even Castro turned away, leaving the dirty business of executing Guerra to his men. Che, however, was up to the task. "Just then a heavy storm broke and the sky darkened," Che wrote later. He pulled out his .32 caliber pistol, put it to Guerra's head, and shot him dead.

This was not the last time Che would prove that he would do what he thought was necessary to win the struggle. Gone was the young romantic who rode his motorcycle in search of carefree adventure and the social idealist who had argued in cafés. He was not even a doctor any longer. He was a man who would kill whomever he thought necessary to defeat what he saw as the oppressive capitalist governments in Cuba and throughout Latin America. He had chosen his bullets over medicine.

Che was ready to put the revolution above his own life and the lives of others. In retrospect, a question hangs over the reputation of Che Guevara: What did he love more, the rebel cause or the violence and killing? He would grow to relish the legend of Che Guevara, the man willing to risk everything and anyone to win the struggle against capitalist oppression. Time would reveal, however, that his ruthlessness would not stop when power was seized. Che was determined to eradicate opposition and to institute worldwide revolution. This was more important than any single individual's life, even his own.

SIX

TRIUMPH

Batista, and the larger world, was beginning to realize that Castro's little army was not merely a band of disorganized insurgents. Batista had claimed victory in the first battles. When reports reached Havana of the army's defeat at La Plata and Arroyo del Infierno, American newspaper reporters took a keener interest in Castro. The regime had made another mistake by reporting that Castro, Che, and Raúl had been killed. Reporters began to doubt the truthfulness of Batista's government.

Herbert Matthews of the *New York Times* was the first journalist to prove Castro was still alive. Posing as a wealthy businessman inspecting a plantation for possible purchase, Matthews visited the Sierra Maestra camp and spent hours talking with Castro. Castro displayed all of his charm and charisma, portraying himself and his soldiers as noble underdogs, outmanned but sure of victory.

"Fidel Castro, the rebel leader of Cuba's youth, is alive and fighting hard and successfully in the rugged, almost impenetrable fastnesses of the Sierra Maestra . . .

Fidel, flanked by his brother Raúl (left) *and Camilo Cienfuegos* (right) *in their camp in the Sierra Maestra, March 1957.* (AP Photo)

President Fulgencio Batista has the cream of his army around the area, but the army men are fighting a thus-far losing battle to destroy the most dangerous enemy General Batista has yet faced in his long and adventur-ous career as a Cuban leader and dictator," Matthews wrote in the most influential paper in the U.S. These were glowing words; Matthews had been charmed. He even wrote about the flash of Castro's eyes and his engaging earnestness.

Castro's skill at manipulating the press helped turn him into a legend. His men, particularly Che, also ad-mired Castro, although they saw a side of him that was not revealed to newspaper reporters. Castro could be a harsh commander. He once berated Che and confiscated his pistol because Che had stashed his rifle on the way to a meeting at a safe house to keep from being recog-nized as a rebel.

Che later wrote that the goal of the Matthews inter-view was for the reporter to give "a full account to the world—especially Cuba—of our existence in the Sierra Maestra and the assurance that Fidel was alive."

Batista claimed the interview was a hoax, which led to more speculation that he was either a liar or hope-lessly out of touch. As the revolution gained momentum, Castro granted several interviews. This led to an obvious question: If well-known reporters could find Castro, why couldn't the Cuban army?

In the interviews Castro was vague about his inten-tions once the revolution was over and he was in power.

He described his politics as nationalistic and democratic, socialist but certainly not Communist. He seemed to many to be a more romantic and vital proponent of the democratic socialism that could be found in Western Europe.

The war was being fought in the cities as well as in the mountains, where peasants sometimes helped guerrillas with food and information. Frank País and Celia Sanchez were among the anti-Batista activists who helped organize riots in the cities. The risks they took, and the price they paid, including capture and torture, were as great as those incurred by the mountain rebels. País sent a group of recruits from the city of Santiago to the rebels in the mountains, reminding the peasant fighters that they had comrades throughout Cuba.

In late May, Che and Castro argued over what were the best targets for attack. Che wanted to strike an army patrol with attack-and-retreat tactics. Castro insisted on assaulting the garrison at El Uvero on the Caribbean Coast. He wanted to prove his army could not only hit and run but prevail in a conventional battle against Batista's trained forces. Castro refused to be swayed by Che's arguments.

On the morning of May 28, eighty rebels split into nine squads encircled the garrison at El Uvero. Castro fired the first shot from a telescopic rifle into the barracks and the rebels immediately opened fire, catching the soldiers inside off-guard. However, the soldiers quickly recovered and began to return fire. Castro ordered his men out of the forest and they advanced forward over open ground. Che crawled on his belly, bullets flying from an enemy trench sixty yards away. For two hours, the barracks soldiers kept the rebels pinned down in a furious firefight. To take pressure off guerrillas in the center, Che decided to mount an attack on the enemy's exposed right flank.

But before he could launch the attack, the battle was over. A white flag appeared above the garrison wall. The regular army had surrendered to a small band of rebels. Seven guerrillas were dead, compared to fourteen regular army soldiers. Fourteen of Batista's troops were taken prisoner, while six escaped.

Castro had proven his point. His rebel army had shown itself capable of prevailing in both guerrilla strikes and head-on combat. After the battle, Castro quickly retreated before army reinforcements arrived. Che followed in a truck loaded with the wounded, including some enemy soldiers, whom Che treated.

The battle of El Uvero brought Castro and Che into closer agreement on battle tactics. The victory in a conventional battle had made an impression, but when it was over Castro had been unable to hold the garrison because of his lack of men. Clearly, they would have to rely on guerrilla tactics for the most part. Castro also respected Che's manifest ability as both a trainer and leader in battle. Together they were putting together a rebel force that would make the Cuban Revolution one of the century's most impressive guerrilla campaigns.

Raúl Castro (left) *poses with his arm around second-in-command, Che Guevara, in their Sierra de Cristal stronghold south of Havana, during the revolution in June 1958.* (AP Photo/Andrew St. George)

Castro rewarded Che in a dramatic way. When the officers signed a condolence letter for the family of a compatriot killed by Batista's troops, Che wrote his name on the left column of the document. When he started to put his rank on the right side, Castro said "Put down Comandante." Che was now only second to commander-in-chief Castro. He later described this as the happiest moment of his life. Officially, Castro designated him the "Comandante of the Fourth Column," but in reality there was no such column. It was a ruse to create the impression that the rebel force was larger than it was.

Fighting continued throughout 1957. Batista's soldiers were unable to pin the rebels down as Castro relied more heavily on Che's guerrilla tactics. As his army suffered and grew frustrated, Batista's grasp on political power began to slip. Earlier that year students from the University of Havana attacked the presidential palace. They stormed past well-armed guards and made their way to Batista's office on the second floor before being stopped. It was a humiliating psychological blow to the regime. Batista shut down the university in November, which only hardened the students' resistance.

Batista's counterattacks often damaged his cause more than the guerrillas were able to do with their small force. When his army went after the guerrillas in the Sierra Maestras, they drove peasants from their land, purportedly to remove them from danger. But many of the peasants feared the evacuations were actually land confiscations.

Che did not hesitate to issue and carry out death sentences on suspected turncoats and informers, although he tried to temper his reputation for ruthlessness with displays of his commitment to loyal rebel fighters. He helped teach illiterate soldiers, and even some enemy prisoners, to read. But his primary goal was to win at any cost. When a deserter or traitor was shot he forced the guerrillas to view the bodies as a warning.

Batista's inability to drive the rebels from the mountains meant they soon had a relatively safe base from which to launch attacks and to spread their message. At

the camp called El Hombrito, Che set up a radio tower
and a mimeograph machine. "Radio Rebelde" broadcast
messages about socialism to the Cuban people, and the
crude printer was used to put out a newspaper. *El Cuba
Libre* (The Free Cuban) published front-page editorials
denouncing Batista and predicting victory for the rebels.

Along with military victories, the message of the
rebels was beginning to take hold. It was helped by the
deepening corruption of Batista's regime. As the rebels
denounced the inequality in Cuba, American mobsters
raked in profits from their hotels and casinos, handing
out generous cuts to Batista and his lieutenants. In 1959,
while Batista's army battled the guerrillas, the dictator
went into partnership with American gangster Meyer
Lansky to build the lavish Hotel Riviera.

The rebels' broadcasts and underground newspaper
reminded the populace of the regime's brutality, and the
police proved their point on an almost daily basis. In
July, the police murdered urban leader Frank País. Protests erupted throughout the cities.

The shakiness of Batista's hold on power began to
worry the CIA and the U.S. State and Defense Depart-
ments. They began to debate the best way to deal with
the problem in Cuba. Castro kept U.S. officials off
balance by refusing to be pinned down on his politics,
but the ruse was wearing thin. The government agencies
agreed that Castro posed a likely threat to U.S. interests
but were uncertain on how to deal with him.

Should the U.S. continue to support Batista or dump

him was the overriding question. The CIA favored dumping Batista. He seemed unable to defeat the rebels. They wanted to organize an officers' coup to overthrow the dictator, but as the war dragged on it became harder to find a suitable replacement.

The ongoing conflict did expose one difference between Castro and Che. Gaining power in Cuba was the most important thing to Castro. He was willing to conceal his true principles and ideology if it would help defeat Batista and put him in power. Che, on the other hand, refused to hide his ideology or to compromise it. As the war raged, Castro was able to use Che's idealism as an effective tool and as a counterweight to Castro's pragmatism. He let Che school the guerrillas in the ideas of Marxism and the young man's idealism was inspiring to the men suffering deprivation in the wilds of Cuba. At the same time, Castro kept most of his plans for post-revolution Cuba secret.

Che's confidence in the purity of their revolutionary ideals suffered a blow when some members of the July 26 Movement were willing to accept a compromise to end hostilities. Former president Carlos Prío Socarrás convened a meeting of some dissident members of the July 26 Movement and other political opponents of Batista from the Auténticos and Orthodoxos parties in Miami, Florida. The Miami Pact called for Batista to step down, the constitution to be restored, and the U.S. to withdraw its aid to Batista. It did not mention ending U.S. influence, nor did it address reforming the economic system.

Che saw the Miami Pact as a rejection of communism. It also called for the integration of the guerrillas into the ranks of the regular army. In his view, they were attempting to paper over the conflict without addressing the underlying issues. It infuriated him that a member of the July 26 Movement, Felipe Pazos, who had been sent to the U.S. to raise money, signed the agreement on the movement's behalf.

Che had built a new base at La Mesa while Castro kept the camp in the Sierra Maestra. From there he appealed to Castro to refute the Miami Pact and Castro complied, denouncing the pact and assuring Che by letter that he had not authorized Pazos to sign on his behalf. Che wrote that Castro's letter filled him "with peace and happiness. Not for any personal reason, but for what this step means for the Revolution."

In mid-February of 1958 Castro broke a two-month lull in hostilities with an attack on the Pino del Agua army barracks. The rebels mounted a single frontal attack, led by Camilo Cienfuegos at dawn on February 16. Castro did not follow up the attack; instead he spread his guerrillas through the area and patiently waited for opportunities to ambush troops.

This was the tactic the regular army soldiers had come to dread. Later that day, a reconnaissance patrol marched into an ambush and suffered heavy casualties. The rebels inflicted casualties at a rate of about four to one, and captured rifles, machine guns, and rounds of ammunition. When counterattacked by mortar fire and fighter planes, Castro's forces showed the resolve of a mature army, standing their ground.

After the Pino del Agua fiasco, the United States cut off arms sales to Batista. The official reason was Batista's use of U.S. planes and arms against a civil insurrection, which violated treaties calling for their use only against a foreign invasion. Washington had expressed displeasure earlier at Batista's violation of the treaty terms. But Batista's inability to defend his regime could not have been lost on American officials. As Batista's hold on power slipped, discussion in Washington focused on what to expect of a Cuba governed by Castro.

Sensing victory, Castro overplayed his hand, and calling for a general strike against the government. His edict demanded that government officials step down and called for citizens to withhold taxes and to refuse recruitment into the army. But the strike failed, for reasons that perplexed Castro. The Cuban Confederation of Labor, the country's strongest labor union, continued to support Batista. Even more surprising, the Cuban Communist Party failed to support the strike, although it still proclaimed support for Castro.

What Castro had failed to take into account was the strong political bond that Batista had built with labor leaders, going all the way back to his first presidency in the 1940s. As for the Communist Party, Batista had allowed them to operate legally and the party's top leaders had become content to work within confines set by the government, while theoretically supporting

Marxist ideals. Some of the party's leaders prospered under Batista. The editor of the Communist Party newspaper, for example, earned a salary of a thousand dollars a month, a princely sum, while his reporters worked for subsistence wages.

Batista was encouraged by the strike's failure. He began buying arms from the Dominican Republic, partially filling the void left by the withdrawal of United States support. In the spring of 1958, he decided to gamble on what he hoped would be the final assault on Castro and his rebels.

Batista sent a force of ten thousand soldiers into the mountains against approximately three-hundred and fifty rebels. It looked like the kind of mismatched showdown Batista and his supporters had long desired. This time the regular army harbored no illusions of an easy, decisive victory. The rebels knew every place to hide, every vantage point, every trail well-suited for an ambush in the mountains. More importantly, they had learned the value of patience.

In the end the campaign became another blow to Batista, both in terms of propaganda and the number of soldiers lost. When the army retreated in August, it had lost more than a thousand men against only fifty dead guerrillas. Castro, in an effort to deal a final blow of his own, dispersed the rebels throughout the central region of Cuba. Their instructions were to disrupt communication and to cut the island in half.

Che and fellow rebel leader Camilo Cienfuegos led

CHE GUEVARA
extranjero pernicioso y Lider
Comunista expulsado de la
Argentina

CAMILO CIENFUEGOS
Lider Comunista

"Villaclareños"

Estos son los dos hombres que quieren llevar a nuestros jóvenes a la muerte y destruir nuestras riquezas.

Nosotros somos Cubanos y no Rusos.

¡LUCHEMOS CONTRA ELLOS!

JUVENTUD CIVICA CUBANA

This 1958 poster, published by a group called the Cuban Civic Youth, warns residents in the Las Villas region of the danger of Castro's forces. Che is referred to as a pernicious foreigner and Communist leader expelled from Argentina. The poster says, "These are the two men who want to lead our youth to their death and destroy our prosperity. We are Cubans and not Russians. Let's fight against them." (Courtesy of Getty Images.)

their band to the Escambray Mountains in the province of Las Villas. Low on rations, the guerrillas tried to avoid even hit-and-run combat en route to their destination.

But a company of Batista's soldiers followed the hungry rebels as they marched along the Caribbean coast.

On September 14, Che marched directly into an ambush leading his men over a railroad line. For once, Batista's forces had trapped him in a battle he could not escape. The guerrillas fought for two-and-a-half hours with the air force hitting them from above. When Che finally retreated, he was forced to leave behind food, medicine, and documents.

The Cuban military caught up with the guerrillas again a couple of weeks later in a swampy coastal region. Che ordered his men to wait until nightfall before making a move. Batista's commanders, weary of playing cat and mouse, called in air force bombers to pound Che's column. By dusk, the trapped guerrillas were desperately trying to find a way around the two hundred regular soldiers blocking their path.

A rebel lieutenant found a lagoon flanking the enemy line and one hundred and forty men, some of them barefoot, waded the lagoon less than a hundred yards from enemy lines. Batista's forces made no attempt to cut off their watery escape. They apparently thought the water was too deep.

Che chalked their escape up to the demoralized state of Batista's troops, weary of losing to an elusive enemy. The media had made instant legends of the rebels. The Cuban Revolution was a hot news story; journalists clamored for an interview with Castro. Some, having witnessed the abuses of the Batista regime, were sympathetic to the rebels. But even those indifferent to the cause were intrigued by the story and helped to turn Castro, Che, Raúl, and others into near mythical figures.

Even as Che's men retreated in near-desperation, the U.S. worried about what a successful revolution would mean for Cuba and the region. Castro may have hedged his political leanings in interviews, but many in the Eisenhower administration considered him a potential ally of the Soviet Union only ninety miles off the coast of Florida. The United States ambassador to Cuba remarked in frustration that "the Communists are marching through Cuba like Sherman's march to the sea." In reality, on their way to the Escambray Mountains, Che's band ducked several battles because of lack of supplies and overwhelming odds.

But as they traveled the rebels found evidence that they were succeeding in the propaganda war. Their ranks began to swell with volunteers. On October 7, Che's men crossed the Jatibonico River into Las Villas province, an arrival he compared to "the passage from darkness into light." They were now in a mountainous terrain from which they could arouse the most fear in their enemies. There they regrouped and made new attacks, dynamiting the Central Highway bridge and railroads linking Havana and Santa Clara.

While fighting near the Escambray range, Che met a woman rebel who would change his life. Aleida March had fought against the government, managing to elude Batista's secret police during several missions despite the thick folder they had compiled on her. The Cuban police had scornfully dubbed her "Scarface" because of a small dog bite she had got on the cheek as a child. In fact, she was blond and pretty.

Aleida's family had once had wealth, but it was gone before Aleida was born. She grew up in the countryside outside the tiny town of Seibaba. Her home was considered comfortable because it had a concrete floor in an area where most houses and even the local school had dirt floors. Her father and mother sharecropped land the family had once owned.

Despite her hardships, Aleida earned good grades and went on to study at the University of Santa Clara. She had planned to be a teacher, but during her university years Castro launched his assault against the Moncada barracks. Just as Che had put aside his medical career, Aleida transformed from teacher to rebel.

Che's legend was well developed when Aleida first met him, but she initially did not think much of the young commandant. She later described him as "dirty and skinny," and, to her twenty-four-year-old eyes, "old" at the age of thirty.

Che brought Aleida into the camp, a breach of the rules because the battle units were composed of only male guerrillas. It was a heady time for the revolutionaries. Batista's regime seemed to be falling apart; the rebels were winning almost everywhere. Che's men began to suspect a romance was developing between the two. One night, Aleida left her room, unable to sleep. Che drove up in his jeep and stopped. He was on his way to an attack and asked if she wanted to come along. She took him up on the offer.

"And from that moment on," she later told an interviewer, "I never left his side—or let him out of my sight." Aleida's and Che's relationship blossomed so quickly that he seemed to forget that he was a married man with a daughter. Hilda Gadea and Hildita spent the revolution in Peru, the occasional letter from Che their only contact.

Castro wanted to strike, and hopefully end the war, while Batista was reeling. He needed to seize power before military officers or some other group could stage a coup. His old rival, former President Carlos Prío Socarrás, who had financed the *Granma* expedition, still wanted to become president.

Castro ordered his men to take Santa Clara, the capital of the Las Villas province. Control of Santa Clara would bottle up Batista's supply routes in the east, leaving the army troops there without supplies for guns and ammunition. Also, a victory at Santa Clara would give the rebels a clear path to Havana.

Che had built a reputation as a guerrilla commander, but now he needed to change tactics and stage a conventional, showdown battle. He planned to cut off access by both road and train from Havana to Santa Clara and to attack in daylight in order to maintain clear battle lines. He began by taking a series of small towns, gathering arms and supplies along the way.

Che's rebels gained momentum and numbers. Many

of Batista's forces gave up without a fight. Some of the commanders who resisted were attacked, while others faced more subtle coercion. When Che's troops took over the highway outside of the small town of Fomento, for example, he telephoned the commander of the local garrison and demanded his surrender. The commander insisted his soldiers would fight. Che ordered the water to the compound be cut off. After several dry days, the officer gave up his command, along with his weapons and supplies.

When Che's column marched into Placetas, a town thirty miles from Santa Clara, the army retreated into its barracks. The rebels marched through empty streets to the walls of the enemy garrison and opened fire with a round of warning shots. The regular soldiers surrendered and, with nearly cool gun barrels, the rebels took their largest city so far as easily as plucking ripe fruit.

Che set up his command headquarters in Placetas and made plans for a quick assault on Santa Clara. He now wanted the kind of war Batista's officers had sought when the ragtag guerrillas had first landed on the beach, a collision of armies with front lines. He studied maps supplied by a geography professor from the University of Santa Clara and planned for house-by-house fighting.

Rebel lieutenants who had been well trained in guerrilla fighting were surprised at Che's departure from his core tactics. But with momentum on the rebels' side, he decided this uncharacteristic frontal assault would catch the enemy by surprise. He also knew that while a guerrilla-style campaign could demoralize a regular army, it was difficult, if not impossible, to hold onto territory using hit-and-run tactics. In order to win the war, he had always known that at some point they would have to engage in more conventional conflict with fronts, flanking movements, and even house-to-house fighting. Che agreed with Castro that now was the time.

Che wanted to plant his troops at the university on the north side of the city and to make it his headquarters. At daybreak on December 29, he ordered Lieutenant Rogelio Acevedo to lead his men into the city. Acevedo had expected to operate under cover of darkness and questioned whether the guerrillas should hold back until dusk.

"No, no, no," Che replied. "We're going in now."

The time for guerrilla war had ended. Acevedo's troops fought the battle by engaging an armored column of infantry that was supported by tanks as they crossed the railroad tracks into the city. The rebels held their ground against heavy gunfire before pushing the army troops back into the city. Other rebels attacked a barracks in the southeast, trapping the soldiers between them.

Suddenly, Che was faced with an unusual dilemma. He feared the regular army commanders would duck the head-on battle and make lightning attacks, much in the same manner he had conducted the war earlier. Then he located an armored train, twenty-two cars long, that had been set up to provide an exit for Batista's troops if needed. Che set a trap. He ordered bulldozers to rip up a section of track leading out of the city. The long-awaited showdown was at hand.

The streets of Santa Clara were ablaze with urban warfare on the morning of December 29. Airplanes rained bombs while gunfire exploded across main thoroughfares and from alleyways. Citizens ran for their lives as shells blasted the walls of their homes. When the battle was over, rebel fighters had taken control of the government offices and Batista officials had either surrendered or fled.

In the afternoon, Batista's soldiers attempted the retreat Che had expected. They boarded the train for their getaway, but the locomotive traveled only a short distance before reaching the sabotaged rails. The locomotive careened off the tracks and the first three cars went down with it. The rebels fired machine guns and threw Molotov cocktails into the derailed wooden cars, which quickly became raging infernos with the regular troops trapped inside. When Che demanded surrender, the commanding officer agreed.

Sporadic fighting continued for two more days. Finally, the rebels, aided by citizens who had joined their cause, snuffed out the last resistance.

Batista carried out his last official function as dictator, a New Year's party, at the presidential palace. He presided over the festivities long enough to serve his guests a dinner of chicken and rice, then retired to a back room to plan his escape. At midnight he resigned from office, and at two A.M., New Year's Day 1959, Batista and about fifty of his top officials boarded a private plane for the Dominican Republic.

On the morning of January 2, Castro gave the command that signaled the success of the Cuban Revolution. He ordered Che, along with fellow commander Camilo Cienfuegos, to march to Havana. When Che's column began the march that afternoon, exhilaration spread through the ranks. Che shared their joy, but knew that an enormous task lay before them. The guerrillas had proven they could topple a corrupt dictatorship. Now they had to prove they could govern the country.

SEVEN
HIGH EXECUTIONER

Anyone watching the spectacle that took place in Havana on January 8, 1959, would have seen a convincing show of unity among triumphant revolutionaries. Fidel Castro rode into the city in a captured tank with Che Guevara by his side. Both men had been turned into folk heroes by their years of fighting the Batista regime and people lined the streets for a glimpse of them.

No one knew what was going on in Castro's mind, however. He had focused all his efforts on attaining political power and had left the theoretical writing and discussion to others. Even the CIA was unsure if he was Stalinist or a democratic socialist.

Castro proudly entered the city with his top lieutenant, but Che had taken on a mythic status that could conceivably pose a threat to Castro in the future. Before the rally was over, Castro had begun to ease Che out of the spotlight. The rebels had brought the *Granma* to Havana, and everyone wanted to see the guerrillas' commander aboard the ship that had brought him to Cuba. Castro obliged, playing to the cheering crowd. He was accompanied by his loyal brother, Raúl. Che was dispatched to secure a garrison.

While Castro gave a speech at an army base, his words were graced by a sign many were convinced had been sent by a higher power. As he spoke of the new Cuba, a dove landed on his shoulder. People in the crowd gasped, many now certain of Castro's place in their nation's history. As always, Castro's spoke in generalities, promising to defend the country, prevent corruption, punish stealing, and battle illiteracy and hunger, but giving no clear idea of how he would accomplish these ends. By his side stood Camilo Cienfuegos, another hero of the revolution, the most visible secondary commander in the celebration.

In the early days Castro was not even the official leader of Cuba. He had Manuel Urritea, a prominent sympathizer, appointed president. Urritea never held any real power and was simply there for cover so Castro could claim to have no designs on power. Castro insisted he was merely a patriot who had rescued his country from a despot. These claims echoed interviews he had given ever since his days in Mexico City. On February 16, though, Castro removed any doubt about his position in the government when he had himself appointed prime minister.

Fidel gestures to a crowd of several hundred thousand people gathered in front of the presidential palace in Havana, Cuba, shortly after Batista was removed from power. (AP Photo/Harold Valentine)

Castro had seen the first sign of the danger Che might pose to his ambitions back when they were still plotting the revolution. While in prison shortly before the launch of the *Granma*, Che had made no secret of his Marxist beliefs at the very time Castro guarded his political philosophy as carefully as his military plans. Che believed that once they were in power in Cuba, they were duty bound to try to take the revolution to other countries, particularly in Latin America, Africa, and other parts of the so-called Third World.

Cienfuegos became a much more public figure in the days following the rebel triumph than he had been during the war. Castro did not want to frighten the United States into intervention, so he put his most amiable commandant out front. No one among his high command could have shown a more congenial face to the American press. Cienfuegos played baseball, cracked jokes, and even wore a Stetson hat. Castro did not want to alarm the military superpower ninety miles to Cuba's north, which, of course, viewed every regime change through the lens of the Cold War. The U.S. had a long tradition of intervening in Cuban affairs, going back to at least the Spanish-American War.

Che loyally stayed out of the limelight, staying for the most part in the colonial fortress Castro had given him to command at La Cabaña. Previously the home of royalty and powerful military leaders, La Cabaña towered above Havana harbor, perched on a rocky overlook.

After the fanfare ended, Che went back to living much as he had in the camps, although in more lavish surroundings. He still looked like a rebel ready for his next patrol. He wore no medals or insignia on his uniform. His hair, rarely washed, hung to his shoulders, and he sported the scraggly beard he had grown in the Sierra Maestra. When Herbert Matthews, the *New York Times* reporter who had written so glowingly of Castro, came to interview him, Che made no attempt to charm his visitor with small talk or jokes.

Matthews asked Che what he thought the Cuban Revolution had to offer. "The most obvious lesson is that one can battle regular forces with troops composed of peasants, workers and intellectuals," Che replied. "This is a vital lesson in the fight against other dictatorships."

This was exactly the kind of direct talk Castro did not want delivered up to the U.S. press. A reader of the *Times* would naturally wonder what other dictatorships Che had in mind. The U.S. supported several dictators they considered to be bulwarks against Communist expansion. Officials in Washington were still arguing over whether they should have continued to back Batista and worried persistently about the Soviet Union's influence in Cuba and elsewhere.

President Eisenhower was nearing the end of his second term. With the 1960 election approaching, he wanted to set a clear policy for U.S.-Cuba relations that his successors would have to follow. Some officials of the Central Intelligence Agency were urging him to invade the island and overthrow the new government. They were convinced that Castro was a Soviet ally.

Castro and every high Cuban official knew the U.S. government was closely listening to what they said and watching their every move. He decided to tour the

United States in an attempt to reassure its people and leaders. On the trip he called for strong economic ties between the two countries and urged American tourists to visit Cuba. He was a charismatic figure with his powerful build, strong voice, full beard, and military uniform that made him seem as if he had arrived fresh from the front. For all of Castro's success in interviews and live speeches, however, troubling signs still emerged from the island, particularly as ex-Batista officials went on trial for their alleged crimes.

Che took a lead role in carrying out trials and handing down sentences, which often called for executions. He had no qualms about taking on the role of executioner. However, it became awkward in early 1959 when his family flew in from Buenos Aires to see their famous son for the first time in six years. His father kissed the tarmac at the airport, and the family reunited with hugs and tears inside a nearby tunnel. Ernesto Sr. beamed in pride as Che's mother embraced him. Surrounded by former guerrillas, Che escorted his family to the Havana Hilton, getting them rooms several floors below those of Fidel. Ernesto Sr. presented his son with several bottles of Argentine wine and recalled later that Che's eyes "shone upon seeing those bottles." He speculated they reminded Che of "pleasant memories of other happy times" of his youth in Buenos Aires.

Che's current duties were not so carefree. He barely had time to settle his family into their quarters at the Hilton before rushing back to La Cabaña to preside over

Che with his parents at the Havana airport in 1959. (AP Photo)

the tribunals. The walls echoed almost every night with the sound of firing squads.

Not long after the visit from his birth family, Che had a more troublesome reunion when Hilda Gadea and Hildita arrived from Peru. Although Aleida had not spoken publicly of the bond she shared with Che, Hilda soon realized they were lovers. The two women never resolved their animosity, but Hilda accepted reality, and on May 22 she granted Che a divorce. On June 2, he and Aleida were married in a civil ceremony, afterwards holding a reception in the home of one of his bodyguards.

Che had a much closer relationship with Aleida than he had with Hilda. He doted on his second wife, bragged to visitors about her good looks, and even had body-guards repel advances from would-be rivals. Even so, Che dearly loved his first daughter. He got his ex-wife a job in Cuba and she often dropped their daughter off to visit him. He let the little girl play in his office as he prepared the charges that sent people to their deaths.

The trials at La Cabaña began at about eight or nine o'clock at night, with verdicts usually reached by two or three in the morning. The walls of La Cabaña were

Che, age 34, with his bride Aleida, stands before the wedding cake following their marriage in 1959. At the extreme left is Raúl Castro, commander in chief of the armed forces. Next to Raúl stands his wife, Vilma Esping. (AP Photo)

thick, but not enough to muffle the gunshots of the firing squads. Farmers in the area could hear the crack of the guns in the dark of early morning and would remember the sounds for the rest of the lives.

The trials imposed a revolutionary justice, which operated on different rules of procedure and evidence than U.S. courts. The goal was to preserve the new government and to punish members of the Batista regime charged with crimes. Many of those on trial had not held high rank in the Batista regime, for Batista's top officers had escaped. Those who remained were usually from the bottom rungs of his government, and a few were mere bureaucrats. Within their ranks were some hired killers and torturers, but simple peasants who had informed on the rebels also stood among the accused.

Che was cold and efficient when it came to running the proceedings and executing old enemies, but he was not sadistic. He wanted to keep the moral high ground against the new government's former enemies and usually insisted on solid evidence of heinous crimes before declaring death sentences. Relatives of those killed by Batista's men testified in the tribunals, while those who had been tortured were asked to show their scars. Che was concerned about the image these trials presented to those outside Cuba.

The same could not be said of Raúl Castro. Fidel's brother seemed to revel in the killing and earned a reputation as a gleeful butcher. Once, after mopping up token resistance in Santiago, Raúl had a bulldozer cut a trench to serve as a mass grave, lined about seventy men in front of it, and had them shot down with machine guns.

Castro grew uncomfortable with the procedure of holding trials behind the walls of places such as La Cabaña, where the public could not see the proceedings. He wanted to assure the readers of newspapers in the U.S. and other democratic countries that his courts would carry out their business in the open. He began to use a major sports stadium in Havana as a court room so all citizens could see the machinery of justice.

But this openness brought about the very backlash Castro had sought to avoid. Graves of victims of the

Built in the eighteenth century, La Cabaña is located on the elevated eastern side of the harbor entrance in Havana, Cuba. The fortress served as a military base and prison for both Spain and an independent Cuba. The complex is now part of a historical park and houses several museums open to the public. (Library of Congress)

Batista era were being opened every day, and revelations of torture seeped into the Cuban press. A lynch-mob fever gripped much of the Cuban public. The media hyped the hysteria, running front-page news accounts of atrocities next to trial coverage that read like angry opinion columns. Reporters wrote accounts portraying the accused as confirmed villains while their trials were still taking place. Prosecutors called for support from the spectators, who obliged by booing defense arguments and cheering for death sentences. Frequently the crowds wanted more severe sentences than those handed out. The entire spectacle struck many in the foreign press as barbaric.

Several U.S. congressmen accused Castro of staging a bloodbath. The criticism stung. Until then he had carefully concealed not only his intentions but also his opposition to United States policy. He finally unleashed his fury in remarks that contrasted with his previous careful diplomacy. How could a nation that had dropped an atomic bomb on civilians at Hiroshima criticize its newly free neighbor as being bloodthirsty? Where was the U.S. concern for human rights when Batista's men had used the backrooms of jails as torture chambers?

Castro's anger must have become all-consuming, or else the pressure of revealing what he had hidden for so long finally won out over his self-control. He began speaking more recklessly than he ever had to the Americans. He warned that an invasion force of "gringos"— an ethnic slur toward North Americans—would result in

200,000 dead Americans. He added that if Washington officials considered him radical, there were those among his supporters who would make him seem quite moderate, and announced that if anything happened to him his brother Raúl would succeed him. With the memory of Raúl's gleeful machine gun spree in Santiago still fresh, Castro's threat alarmed officials in the White House, Congress, and the CIA.

Che felt no remorse about the trials. While not openly sadistic, he was not particularly inclined toward mercy. When Castro stewed over criticism from the U.S., Che reminded him of what he had seen in Guatemala. President Arbenz had not purged his enemies and, in return for his mercy, had lost his government to a CIA coup.

Those who had known Che as a young man were often surprised at how hard he had become. His father decided to visit him one night at La Cabaña. Che was not there and Ernesto Sr. decided to wait. As he waited, one of the guards fell asleep. Che's jeep arrived shortly afterward. Che got out, walked up to the guard, and yanked the rifle from the sleeping soldier's hands. Che's father saw a look of desperate fear cross the young man's face as Che ordered him arrested for sleeping on duty. His father questioned why it was necessary to be so harsh. "He answered me: 'Old man, nobody here can sleep on guard duty because it puts the whole barracks at danger.'"

Although the Cuban Revolution had ended, Che thought no guerrilla could relax. In his mind, the larger revolution, particularly in the Americas, would continue.

He wanted all of Latin America to undergo a revolution similar to Cuba's and to rid itself of U.S. and capitalist influence. He was convinced that only a grand- scale international revolution had a chance of succeeding in the long term. Communism in one country could never become permanent. While Castro tiptoed around conflicts, Che invited them.

Che did not mince words when he spoke at a Havana forum sponsored by the Popular Socialist Party (PSP), the official Communist party of Cuba. The Communists had failed to support Castro's call for a strike against the government during the revolution, which added to U.S. confusion regarding Castro's stance on communism. Che's speech, titled "Social Projections of the Rebel Army," left little doubt.

Che attacked American corporations for their domination of politics and life in South America and Cuba. Cuba needed to develop a healthy independent economy, he declared, not one dependent on sugar exports. He called for a massive program of industrialization and the expropriation of U.S. assets in Cuba, including the national telephone company, a subsidiary of the American firm ITT. Che also claimed that Cuba was under no obligation to pay companies compensation when it took their property.

The citizens must learn how to operate not only industrial machines but also firearms, he said. The revolution must continue throughout the oppressed countries of South America. He threw down the gauntlet with these words: "The Revolution has put the Latin American tyrants on guard because these are the enemies of popular regimes, as are the monopolistic foreign countries."

While Che sounded like a tiger at the podium, those close to him could see his health was beginning to fray. He was thin and pale, with deep shadows under his eyes. He had suffered a bout of asthma in early March, and a doctor also diagnosed a pulmonary infection, advising Che to move out of the drafty La Cabaña fortress. He and Aleida moved into the house of a former high-ranking Batista official in Tarrará. Self-conscious about taking over the luxurious villa of a former "oppressor," Che nonetheless made the house his new home and headquarters as he continued his writing and planning.

He took over as the informal leader of a group in charge of farm reform, the National Institute of Agrarian Reform (INRA). The group consisted of Che's top lieutenants, other leaders of the July 26 Movement, and, unknown to those outside the villa, members of the PSP. Other than Castro, no one in the central government knew of the INRA's existence. Its main task was to create more jobs in the sugar industry. Hiring in sugar jobs had slowed down, due to concern about the economic stability of the plantations during and after the revolution. Investors prefer to do business in a stable economic environment and were waiting to get a clear sign of the country's ultimate direction. The INRA would also take a central position in overseeing health care, education, and welfare.

Above all, the secret group meeting at Che's temporary home intended to make the revolutionary government permanent. When Che lobbied for a shorter work day to create more jobs, one of the INRA members protested that such a measure would increase production costs. Che agreed, but argued the new government had no choice if they wanted to reduce unemployment. If the workers were not happy, he argued, Castro's government would share the fate of Batista's.

Such details were not as interesting to Che as the military adventures had been, though he knew they were essential to governing. When not arguing over the details of the new economy, Che took the time to write articles for the newspaper *Prensa Latina* (Latin Press) and the magazine *Verde Olivo* (Olive Drab). Most of his work addressed the need for ongoing revolution throughout Latin America and the Third World. He also worked on his first book, eventually titled *Guerrilla Warfare*, a manual for guerrilla fighters.

Castro gave Che a rewarding assignment in June when he sent him on a global goodwill tour. It was the perfect antidote to the bureaucratic planning Che had slogged through with the INRA, and was better suited to his adventuring spirit. He visited Egypt, Yugoslavia, India, Indonesia, and Japan. Everywhere he showed his face, the crowds recognized him, for next to Castro he was the most famous of the Cuban revolutionaries.

When he visited the Soviet Union, however, Che tried to stay out of the public eye. Cuba sought new markets for its sugar, and leaders in Moscow were interested in establishing new ties with the island. But Castro wanted to keep the U.S. in the dark about any Moscow-Havana tics for as long as possible.

Che's found his official travels did less to satisfy his wanderlust than those he had taken as a young man. In Egypt, he wished he could have wandered alone among the pyramids and tombs, unrecognized. At the same time, he felt a sense of his importance in history. He never felt the revolution had ended with Batista's hasty departure. And as a revolutionary he had premonitions of a violent end, feelings he expressed in a letter to his mother. "I feel not just a powerful inner strength, which I've always felt, but as though I'm doing something in life; I feel that I have a capacity to give something to others and an entirely fatalistic sense of my mission, which makes me quite fearless," Che wrote.

Some of Che's closest comrades feared his travel tour amounted to a demotion, but Castro received Che warmly on his return. Che never wavered in his support for Castro, even as some of the other former rebels began to turn against the prime minister.

Castro had to deal with dissent in his first year in office. Huber Matos, a guerrilla commander and leader in the July 26 Movement, accused Castro of giving the Communists too much influence in his government. Matos was angry about proposals to take away land from prominent ranchers, many of whom were his friends. When the government refused to act on his complaints,

Matos resigned and accused Castro of betraying his own ideals. A group of anticommunist officers joined Matos in resignation. Castro accused Matos of treason and had him arrested, tried, and sentenced to more than twenty years in prison.

Pedro Díaz Lanz, Castro's air force chief, also protested the Communist influence in Cuba. He defected to the United States and subsequently gave testimony detailing Castro's links to communism before a Senate committee. Díaz Lanz's vengeance against his former leader was not complete, however. In October of 1959, he flew a B-29 bomber over Havana during a convention of 2,000 travel agents. He dropped leaflets decrying the Communist influence in Havana. Castro's anger at these revolts from within his ranks led to increased vigilance against counterrevolution, which became one of the most dreaded crimes of which one could be accused.

Revolutionary Air Force chief Pedro Díaz Lanz in 1959.

Castro still needed to find an official post for Che, one that would keep his charismatic presence far enough away to prevent the prime minister from being upstaged yet prestigious enough to satisfy Che's followers. The compromise would have amused Che when he was in training as an anticapitalist guerrilla. Castro named him head of the National Bank of Cuba.

A funny story is told about the way Che acquired the post. At a meeting of his top leaders, Castro asked "Is there an economist in the room?"

Che misheard the question. "Communist? Why, of course! Me!" Che had been careful not to use the word "Communist" to describe himself while training the guerrillas because many of the rebels opposed the ideology. In fact, Che considered himself a socialist revolutionary. But the prime minister accepted the self-nomination, so the story goes, and Castro's top guerrilla became Cuba's top banker. Upon hearing of Che's new post, Ernesto Sr. said, "Fidel's crazy. Every time a Guevara starts a business, it goes bust."

Che knew that Cuba needed a way to finance its industrial growth, which would in the long run strengthen the socialist revolution. He studied higher math along with economic theory and practice. He had his limitations as a banker, however, and insisted that revolutionary principles take precedence over policy, a position not exactly in step with most bankers.

The fact Che was not a typical banker was revealed when he signed Cuba's new currency. He simply wrote

"Che." To his intimates, Che's gesture was an inside joke. To his critics it was yet another omen of the threat he presented.

Che again revealed his contempt for banking as a profession when he bickered with architect Nícolas Quintana about the design of the new bank headquarters in Havana. The building was to stand sixty-four stories tall on an island that sometimes took the brunt of Caribbean storms. The architect suggested hurricane-proof glass, the better to protect not only the building but the currency inside. Che said no. "For the [stuff] we're going to be guarding here within three years, it's preferable that the wind take the lot." It was one thing for a rebel to have contempt for money, but quite another for the national bank president. Cuban businesspeople were furious at Che's appointment to the post, as well as his apparent contempt for it.

EIGHT

SHOWDOWN WITH THE U.S.

As 1960 began, Castro showed himself to be capable of public-relations blunders. It was a presidential election year in the U.S., the most sensitive time possible for foreign leaders in delicate negotiations with the United States. Political candidates had to weigh their words carefully, for any careless phrase could set off a full-blown controversy. Castro had usually shown an instinctive understanding of the American media, delivering his message to the American public almost as eloquently as if he had written the stories himself. But he fumbled through the 1960 election as though he knew nothing of the U.S. electoral process.

Some American owners of Cuban property had lost their plantations to Castro's agrarian reforms and were clamoring for compensation. American companies had also received nothing from the Cuban government for their lost property. When the U.S. State Department asked Castro for payment for the landowners he had dispossessed, he responded by seizing the remainder of American plantations, even though he knew that governments that seized land from the affluent were almost always identified as Communist in American politics.

For a leader still trying to remain officially neutral in the standoff between the U.S. and the Soviet Union it was a remarkably reckless move. The election year would have been an excellent time to stay out of the American limelight. Instead, Castro turned himself into one of the central issues of the campaign.

Republican candidate, Vice President Richard Nixon had met with Castro in 1959 and reported to President Eisenhower that Castro was a Communist. Still, he argued, Castro might also be politically naïve and, "[B]ecause he has the power to lead, we have no choice but to at least try to orient him in the right direction."

Going in the "right direction" (or pretending to) might have allowed Castro to continue playing the middleman in the U.S.-Soviet conflict for an extended time. While such a strategy would have displeased the idealistic Che, Castro had always been able, and willing, to restrain his impulses.

But Castro began to startle many in the U.S. and Europe. Before a live television audience he accused Spain of helping to smuggle his opponents out of the country. The Spanish ambassador to Cuba, Juan Pablo de Lojendio, stormed into the studio to interrupt Castro's speech, protesting that it was all lies. De Lojendio began to yell at Castro as he was escorted out of the studio. Castro then began a tirade against the United States.

Why Castro chose to turn on the U.S. is still debated. The Soviets might have given him enough assurances on trade and assistance that he now felt comfortable enough to drop any pretense of working with Americans. Che might have delivered such Soviet promises after his return from the global goodwill trip. Even so, a more seasoned leader might have taken a lower profile.

Castro's speech, combined with other open rebukes of the U.S., led to the recall of the American ambassador in Havana. Secretary of State Christian Herter had dined with Castro the year before, when Castro appeared to be seeking closer ties with the U.S., and found the Cuban leader amiable and charming. Now Herter appeared before Congress to ask for presidential authority to limit Cuban sugar purchases.

Castro became a topic in the U.S. elections. The controversy was less about what policy to take toward Cuba than about which candidate, and party, would be the toughest on Castro. Charges flew between Republican nominee Nixon and the Democratic nominee, Senator John Fitzgerald Kennedy, over who was "soft on Castro."

As challenger, Kennedy was able to gain the most ground. President Eisenhower was willing to enforce the sugar quotas, but he did not favor immediate military action. Vice President Nixon had to maintain the administration's official line, leaving Kennedy free to ratchet up the rhetoric. The Massachusetts senator spoke openly of overthrowing Castro and accused the Eisenhower administration of doing nothing.

Both candidates knew better. The Central Intelligence Agency had briefed the nominees on its anti-Castro plans, which were quite advanced. Using unmarked planes, the CIA had been flying spy missions over Cuba in preparation for an invasion. Castro suspected he was being targeted for a U.S.-sponsored overthrow, as did Che. He might have known that the CIA was using Guatemala as a training ground for an invasion force of anti-Castro Cubans and CIA agents. Ironically, in the country where Che had developed his policy of standing tough against enemies of the revolution, the same CIA that had toppled President Arbenz was now preparing for a new attack, this time in Cuba.

Even as President Eisenhower sought to ease tensions, Castro held a Soviet trade fair in Cuba that flashed images of the friendly Soviet-Cuban relationship around the world. At the fair, the Soviets displayed a replica of their greatest triumph in space, the Sputnik satellite, along with models of homes, factories, and farm equipment.

Soviet Deputy Premier Anastas Mikoyan attended the fair with his son Sergo. An eavesdropping Sergo got an interesting and unguarded view of both Castro and Che. He found Castro to be self-absorbed, more interested in talking about his own agenda than listening to others. Che's mystique had Sergo expecting to meet a fiery and volatile radical, but he discovered the opposite in Che: "Although I had expected him to be the obstinate one, I realized he wasn't stubborn, but inclined to talk, to discuss and to listen."

Che did not keep his mouth shut when the discussion turned on matters he considered critical. Castro and Che made a candid confession to Deputy Premier Mikoyan that laid bare their long-running intentions. They needed Russia's aid to survive but had to keep it as secret as possible for some time.

The two differed dramatically, however, on the time-table. Castro said it would take as much as five more years before Cuba could become an openly socialist state. Sergo recalled, ". . . Che interrupted and told him: 'If you don't do it within two or three years, you're finished.'"

A disaster soon lent weight to Che's argument that Cuba would have to tip its hand sooner rather than later. At about 3 P.M. on March 4, 1960, the French freighter *La Coubre* exploded in the Havana harbor. Police and firefighters arrived quickly on the scene, in time for many of them to be killed in a second explosion. *La Coubre* had been carrying munitions for Castro's army.

Castro quickly blamed the CIA for sabotaging the ship. U.S. officials said that the Cuban workers had been careless while handling the explosive materials. No one was able to determine what really happened, but the incident became the spark which ignited the Cold War conflict between the U.S. and Cuba.

Castro decided to seek Soviet military aid, which was readily granted. Oil shipments from the USSR began arriving in April. In May, Cuba announced it would commence diplomatic relations with the Soviet Union. The Soviet Union also began to secretly send arms to the island, working to avoid CIA detection. Castro's actions quickened the exodus of affluent Cubans to the U.S. as Che and others talked frequently about redistribution of wealth.

At the memorial service for _La Coubre,_ photographer Alberto "Korda" Diaz took one of the most famous photos of Che. Standing behind Castro, handsome in his full beard and black beret with gold star, Che stares resolutely, eyes shining with grim resolve. Outside Cuba, people read different messages from Che's expression. Some saw the cold threat of a would-be dictator; others viewed him as an idealist and revolutionary. The photo became a part of Che's mystique, one of the images that came to symbolize revolution in the 1960s.

Che used his position as head of the national bank to pressure the United States. Cuba had fallen into debt to American-owned oil companies. He offered to let the U.S. oil companies in Cuba process the newly arriving Soviet oil in exchange for their forgiveness of the debt. At the height of the Cold War, it is doubtful Che seriously expected the American companies to accept an offer to help process oil delivered from the Soviets. The offer was probably intended to outrage them. When the oil companies rejected his offer, Che ordered them nationalized.

Fashion photographer Alberto "Korda" Diaz entitled his 1960 image of Che "The Heroic Guerrilla." (AP Photo)

Washington retaliated by suspending all purchases of Cuban sugar. Because it was Cuba's major purchaser of sugar, the loss of the U.S. market severely hurt the

Cuban economy. The Soviet Union stepped in to fill the gap; Soviet Premier Nikita Khrushchev offered to buy the surplus. Khrushchev underscored his support of the Cuban regime by boldly declaring that he would also send missiles if needed.

As Cuba strengthened its bonds with the Soviet Union, Che began to speak on television and at universities about his vision for a new ideal of economic life. He called for the creation of "the new man," a worker who would labor out of a sense of duty and for the good of society rather than for material gain.

Che admitted it was impractical to scrap all material incentives at once, but sought to relegate them to secondary status. He set an example by laboring during his own off-hours, helping to cut sugar cane and build government buildings and schools. His fame may have helped morale in the cane fields, but even Cubans loyal to Castro were slow to embrace the idea of working for moral satisfaction alone.

The United States knew how to use and manipulate material incentives. In October 1960 the Eisenhower administration imposed a blockade on Cuban goods. It began negotiations concerning Cuba with the Organization of American States (OAS), an organization formed in 1948 in cooperation with the United Nations for the purpose of coordinating economic, political, and military matters in the region. The U.S. persuaded the OAS to issue a statement condemning joint aggression by Cuba and the Soviet Union. The United States also threatened to cancel foreign aid to any country that purchased Cuban sugar.

Both presidential candidates promised vigilance against any Soviet presence in Cuba. Because the Batista regime had fallen during Eisenhower's watch, however, Nixon was in a tight spot. Kennedy seized the political advantage by painting the Eisenhower administration as weak in its dealings with Castro. Although there were many factors at play in the election, Kennedy won the presidency in 1960 by one of the slimmest margins ever.

Just as Kennedy took office in January of 1961, Che was taking on a new job as well. He became the minister of industry. He privately complained about having to

Although plans for the attempted overthrow of Castro's government were in motion before John F. Kennedy took office, the new U.S. president was largely responsible for the botched effort that became known as the Bay of Pigs invasion. (Library of Congress)

take the job. He was never happy in bureaucratic positions. The battles with Batista had transformed him into a guerrilla. He confided to friends that he could last no more than five years in the post before seeking a new revolution.

Before dawn on April 15, 1961, the Guevara household woke to the sound of airplanes and explosions. Che ran shirtless to the window and watched as unmarked planes dropped bombs on the nearby Campamento Libertad airfield. His men ran in a disorganized melee outside, brandishing their pistols. Che opened the window and shouted for them to settle down.

He already had his orders for defense of the island, for the invasion had long been suspected and even reported as imminent by Castro's spies. Che drove to the Pínar del Rio military zone, where Castro had ordered him in the event of an invasion, where he rallied his troops with the cry "Homeland or death!"

The first wave of the attack succeeded despite their preparations. The B-26 bombers' strike wiped out most of Castro's air force and left many casualties. At the funeral for those killed in the attack, Castro erased all uncertainty about the final nature of the Cuban Revolution. He blamed the United States for the deaths and declared that the revolution had been a victory for socialism.

The second wave of the U.S.-led invasion came two days later, when fifteen-hundred mostly Cuban armed men, who had been trained by the CIA and called themselves the Liberation Army, landed at Playa Gíron on the Bay of Pigs. Castro's forces swarmed to the landing site and pinned down the invasion force. The invasion bogged down as the Liberation Army awaited reinforcements that never came. The would-be liberators did not get support from the air as they had expected. Confusion turned to fear as Castro's army closed in.

The mission had been poorly planned in Washington. The troops who had trained in Guatemala had been mostly former pro-Bastista exiles. The Americans wanted

The locations of the invading forces in April 1961 are marked on this map. Castro said one invasion force struck in the southern part of Las Villas Province (1). Another force was reported ashore at the edge of southern Matanzas Province in the Cochinas Bay area (2). Other reported landings took place in the Western Pinar Del Rio Province (3), Baracoa (4), northeast of Santiago, in the Matanza Province (5), and the Santiago area (6), with parachutists dropped on the Isle of Pines (7). (AP Photo)

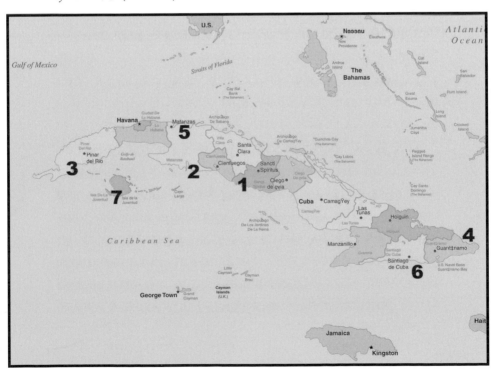

the invasion to seem like a rebel force similar to the one Castro led against Batista. They wanted the world to see Cubans regaining control of their island from a repressive regime, not a U.S. invasion. But their CIA instructors had misled them with a combination of bravado and ignorance. The agency organizers also kept vital information secret from the natives of the island who were supposed to serve as the vanguard of the attacking force. The invaders did not know where they would land or where they would go afterwards. The CIA had planned for the Liberation Army to move quickly to a "nearby" mountain range, but the mountains they chose for cover were the Escambray Mountains, over a hundred miles away. They promised the fighters they would be joined by sympathizers inside Cuba; none arrived. They promised air cover, but the president had not authorized any. Despite the success of a first air strike, an indecisive President Kennedy did not order a second wave, which was even more important because it was to come after troops had landed. With no air support, the mission was doomed.

Five days after it landed, the invasion fell to pieces. The Cuban Army killed one hundred and fourteen Liberation Army soldiers and took prisoner another twelve hundred. The cost to the U.S. was staggering; the four-billion-dollar budget for the invasion mushroomed to 46 billion. Castro used the prisoners for both propaganda and ransom. The U.S. eventually had to buy their release for 62 million dollars in medical supplies.

In military, financial, and political terms, the invasion was a fiasco for the U.S. In a later face-to-face meeting with Richard Goodwin, a Kennedy aide, Che dryly "thanked" the U.S. for the gift of the Bay of Pigs.

Not all of America's efforts to thwart Cuba failed, however. The blockade it had organized had shut down seventy-five percent of its trade with other countries. Che attempted to use his power as the minister of industry to keep the economy running, but he faced obstacles on every front. State farms operated with outdated machinery and the factories ran with equally threadbare equipment. The blockade forced Cuba to ration food and household supplies.

Che and Aleida eventually had four children: two sons, Ernesto and Camilo, and two daughters, Aliusha and Celia. Aleida enjoyed parties and movies, while Che cared little for amusements. He worked long hours and spent his little leisure time reading. The danger they had shared during the revolution had sealed their bond, however, and they agreed on almost every aspect of philosophy and politics. Like Che, Aleida spoke her mind candidly, unconcerned with whom she might offend. Not least, Che never lost the physical attraction that he felt for her. Even in front of visitors to their home, he made sly allusions to her physical charms.

Che and Aleida tried to set a good example by making sure they had no more meat or milk than the workers, but Che's diligence about maintaining the restrictions did cause family friction. When a friend sent her a pair of

This photograph of Guevara with his wife, Aleida, and their four children portrays an image of Che very different from his brutal revolutionary persona. (AP Photo)

expensive Italian shoes, he made her return them on the grounds that ordinary women could not afford such luxuries. When the children got sick, he would not allow her to use his official car because it was strictly for use in the business of "the people." He told her to take them by bus like everyone else. Che's stinginess with his family became so well-known that a sympathetic Soviet official slipped hors d'oeuvres into Aleida's purse at a diplomatic reception.

While the few precious hours he spent at home were satisfying, he chaffed at his bureaucratic duties. He felt his real talents lay on the battlefield. For a while, he had to be content to fight the war with words, such as when he traveled to a conference on President Kennedy's Alliance for Progress, a program that attempted to build links between the U.S. and Latin America by providing 20 billion dollars of economic aid. Kennedy wanted to counter Soviet and Cuban influence in the region by providing money for schools and roads. The U.S. most often judged Latin American countries in the light of the Cold War. President J. M. Velasco Ibarra of Ecuador, for example, was judged hostile to the U.S. primarily because he was considered to be friendly with Castro. When he was overthrown in 1961, many of his countrymen suspected CIA involvement. Brazil drew complaints from the U.S. simply by trying to stay neutral. Kennedy praised the military junta of El Salvador for its effectiveness in containing communism. Che argued that no democracy created by the United States would be authentic because it would be ensnared in U.S.-style capitalism.

At an Alliance for Progress meeting in Uruguay in August of 1961, Che warned delegates from other countries that they were in danger of being manipulated by "politicians dressed up as [economic] experts." He bluntly told the assembly they would be hoodwinked if they let their countries accept aid or loans with strings attached.

"Don't you get a slight feeling your leg is being pulled?" Che goaded. "Dollars are given to build highways, dollars are given to build sewers. Gentlemen, what are highways and roads built with, what are sewers built with, what are houses built with? You don't have to be a genius to answer that. Why don't they give dollars for equipment, dollars for machinery, dollars so that all of our underdeveloped countries, all of them, may become industrial-agricultural countries at one and the same time? It really is sad."

Che insisted the Alliance for Progress's real purpose was for the U.S. to dilute Cuban influence. However, he did attempt to placate the Americans by promising that Cuba would give a "guarantee that we shall not export revolutions, we guarantee that not a single rifle will leave Cuba, that not a single weapon will leave Cuba for battle in any other country of America."

Che was being at least as deceptive as Kennedy. Nothing was closer to his heart than his dream of world-wide Communist revolution. If the Americans were trying to contain the ideology with the Alliance of Progress, Che was equally as determined to spread it.

The Soviet Union was also seeking to extend its influence in Cuba and the Americas in a highly danger-ous way. Soviet Premier Nikita Khrushchev thought the future of communism could be in Cuba. If he allowed the U.S. to overthrow Castro, either by subterfuge or by direct invasion of U.S. troops, he and the Soviet Union would lose credibility with other pro-Communist gov-ernments and guerrilla groups. He planned a bold move to prove to the world that the Soviet Union would do what was necessary to defend Communist governments any-where in the world.

Khrushchev told Che and Castro that he wanted to

install nuclear missiles in Cuba. Raúl Castro went to Moscow to sign a treaty in which the Soviets agreed to come to Cuba's defense, even if it meant nuclear war. The USSR would also put forty-two thousand soldiers in Cuba, along with the forty-two nuclear missiles.

Initially, Castro was cagy about accepting the Soviet proposal. Che argued strongly in favor of accepting the missiles and the base. "Anything that can stop the Americans is worthwhile," he argued.

The Cubans and Russians haggled over the terms of the deal. The Russians planned to keep full control over the missiles and troops. Khrushchev insisted they would be used only as a last resort. But Castro and Che were adamant that the Soviet Union make a stronger commitment to Cuba's defense. They did not want Cuba to become merely a Soviet launching pad. They insisted the Soviet Union sign an agreement declaring that any attack on Cuba would be considered an attack on the Soviet Union. Khrushchev agreed. Even as Raúl Castro wrapped up the final bargaining sessions in Russia, Soviet cargo ships began sailing toward Cuba. The world was on the verge of the most dangerous confrontation of the Cold War.

Khrushchev knew 1962 was a congressional election year in the United States. He wanted to be more careful than Castro had been in 1960 and keep the base a secret until the November ballots were cast. But U.S. U-2 spy planes photographed clear evidence of the missiles, and on October 16 intelligence officials showed photos to

Kennedy that revealed missiles, tracks and dollies for transporting them, and storage areas. The evidence was indisputable.

The range of the missiles varied from thirteen-hundred to twenty-five hundred miles. Apprehension turned to anger as Kennedy and his advisers pored over the photographs. The Soviets could launch an atomic attack on any city in the United States from Cuba. The president ordered military commanders to move troops within striking distance of Cuba and to prepare for an invasion.

On October 22, Kennedy went on television and told the American public of the danger the nation faced. He described the discoveries made by the spy planes, leaving no doubt that the U.S. now had an enemy missile base less than a hundred miles from its shores. The president had wanted to impose a military blockade against Cuba, but aides advised him that would technically be an act of war because it would stop every ship entering or leaving the country. (The earlier embargo was intended to stop trade between the U.S. and Cuba.) Kennedy instead called his response to the missiles a "quarantine." The U.S Navy would encircle Cuba and block any Soviet ship that tried to pass, he said, and would board the ships to check for weapons.

Then Kennedy stated that if the Soviet Union launched any missiles from Cuba the U.S. would make a "full retaliatory response." Kennedy's speech raised the specter of a worldwide nuclear holocaust.

Kennedy's words frightened people throughout the

A view of the bed where Che slept during the Cuban Missile Crisis at his headquarters in a grotto near Pinar del Rio, Cuba. Che and Soviet authorities had meetings in this cave in Oct. 1962, a few miles from where missiles were positioned. (AP Photo/Jose Goitia)

world. Che welcomed the conflict. He was sure the U.S. would invade Cuba again anyway, and the missiles gave Cuba a new edge in the inevitable conflict. On October 23, Castro dispatched Che to Pinar del Río on the western coast of Cuba, considered a likely invasion point for U.S. troops, where he quickly began stockpiling weapons and rallying his soldiers. He claimed to hope the Americans would invade soon.

The invasion was not to come. Instead, Castro and Che would get a lesson in superpower diplomacy. Kennedy's threat had rattled Khrushchev. He knew the U.S. had nuclear missiles in Turkey that could target

Moscow and other population centers in the Soviet Union. Khrushchev had apparently considered Kennedy too naïve and too young (Kennedy was only forty-four when inaugurated) to be an effective leader, and the Bay of Pigs fiasco had seemed to confirm his judgment. But here he was openly threatening nuclear war if the missiles were not removed, and he seemed resolute. Soviet leaders argued furiously about what to do the whole day after Kennedy's speech.

Khrushchev delivered his response in a private message on October 26. He agreed to take the missiles out of Cuba if Kennedy removed U.S. missiles from Turkey and pledged not to invade the island. Khrushchev shortly thereafter made a public speech outlining the same terms.

While the U.S. and Soviet Union tried to find a way out of the situation without losing face, Cuban troops prepared for invasion. On October 27 they shot down a U-2 plane, killing the pilot. Kennedy downplayed the incident, still hoping for a diplomatic solution, although he refused Khrushchev's first offer. With the memory of the Bay of Pigs fresh in his mind, Kennedy was determined not to appear to weak in the eyes of the world. He dispatched his brother, Attorney General Robert Kennedy, to the Soviet embassy in Washington with a counteroffer. The U.S. would withdraw its missiles from Turkey but would not concede that their withdrawal was conditional upon the Soviets removing their missiles from Cuba. The Russians would have to keep the Turkey compromise a secret or the deal was off.

Khrushchev blinked. On October 28, he announced the Soviet Union would take its missiles out of Cuba if the U.S. pledged not to invade. The Soviet premier's reputation was damaged by agreeing to keep the removal of the missiles from Turkey secret. To most of the world, it appeared Khrushchev had simply folded under pressure.

Che and Castro shared that view. Castro was particularly incensed that Khrushchev had not told him about the agreement in advance. He heard about the withdrawal like most other people, by listening to the radio. After hearing the speech, Castro smashed a mirror with his fist.

Che was equally disgusted. Soviet leaders had courted him on his visits to Russia, but he now held them in contempt for avoiding conflict with the United States. He told a British reporter that if he had been in charge the missiles would have been launched. He would never again trust the Soviet Union and longed more than ever to take matters into his own hands.

NINE
FAILED REBELLIONS

After the Cuban Missile Crisis, which Che viewed as an ignoble defeat for world communism, he began to look for a new place to fight. It was necessary, he said, to keep the tide of revolution on the move. One of the nations where he thought a socialist rebellion could be engineered was Argentina.

The political conditions in Argentina were chaotic. In August of 1961, over a year before the Cuban Missile Crisis, President Arturo Frondizi requested a meeting with Cuba in an attempt to establish more cordial relations. Frondizi also wanted assurance that Cuba would make no formal military pact with Moscow. Castro sent Che to meet the Argentine president. Che assured Frondizi that Cuba would not join in any Soviet military action against the U.S. unless the United States attacked Cuba.

After their lunch, Che visited a sick aunt in Buenos Aires and then flew home.

Being seen with Che, however, could be the kiss of death for a foreign leader. Anticommunist military leaders made their displeasure over the meeting known, and the press printed critical stories about President Frondizi's meeting with the most famed guerrilla leader of the Americas. Frondizi's foreign minister made things worse by first denying Che's visit, which triggered a scandal that forced the minister to resign when the news leaked out. Seven months later, a military coup drove Frondizi from office.

There were problems within the Communist world as well that hindered Che's dream of spreading the ideology throughout the world. The biggest problem was the growing rift between the Soviet Union and China. China's Communist guerrilla leader Mao Zedong had enjoyed good relations with Russia when he came to power in 1949. Premier Joseph Stalin of the USSR had been one of Mao's early allies. Stalin was a brutally harsh leader, however, and when Nikita Khrushchev ascended to power he wanted to purge the Soviet Union of Stalin's influence. He aroused the suspicions of the Chinese leaders in 1956 when he denounced his former boss's excesses. In China, Stalin was still revered for supporting Mao at a time when leaders of the Western democracies scorned him. Also, Khrushchev rejected some of Stalin's Marxist-Leninist core principles, including the belief that armed conflict between socialist and capitalist nations was inevitable. Mao shared this belief. Khrushchev's botched handling of the Cuban Missile Crisis only further eroded his standing with Mao Zedong and his followers.

Relations between the former allies grew steadily worse through the late 1950s and early 1960s. Khrushchev alarmed the Chinese when he held a summit with President Dwight Eisenhower in 1959. The Soviet Union had earlier promised to help China develop nuclear weapons, but Khrushchev reneged on this promise. When China and India clashed in a border dispute, the Soviets backed India, a country that had pursued friendly relations with the USSR.

Che had visited Mao on his trip to China. The two men became friendly, in part due to Mao's experiences as a guerrilla leader. As Russia and China drifted farther apart, Che became identified as the Cuban most friendly to China. The Soviets grew suspicious of him, and even assigned an agent from their spy agency, the KGB, to monitor him.

All this came at a time when Castro was trying repair relations with the USSR. The Russians' handling of the missile affair had angered Castro, but he needed their support more than ever. Also, Castro wanted the Soviets to help launch a socialist rebellion in Argentina. It was the USSR, not China, which had supplied Cuba with arms and supplies. But a rebellion in Che's native country was not high on the Soviets', or the Chinese's, list of priorities. As it turned out, it was not high on the list of a majority of Argentinians, either.

Che with Chairman Mao Zedong during his visit to China in 1964. (AP Photo)

Che struggled at the ministry of industry. He still wanted Cuba to become an industrial power, but the U.S. embargo undercut his efforts. Few were willing to embrace his ideal of the selfless "new man." Che could labor in the cane fields and work sixteen-hour days, but most common workers did not try to match his intensity.

Che's reputation as a harsh leader grew as he dealt with the lax attitudes of industry ministry workers. He set up a "rehabilitation camp" at a remote, hot, and barren section of western Cuba. Camp Guanacahabibes was a name that came to be dreaded. Anyone who committed what Che considered moral errors—trying to cover up mistakes, for examples, or having affairs with married women—were called before Che and given a

Raúl poses with Che in Mexico City during the Cuban anniversary meeting, July 26, 1964. (AP Photo/Jesus Diaz)

choice. They could either be fired or take a sentence of hard labor for up to a year at Camp Guanacahabibes.

Even his closest aides had to watch their step. When a new bodyguard polished Che's boots, Che denounced him as a "brown-noser" and kicked him in the buttocks. The angry guard then threw Che's boots in the street, thus losing a week's worth of wages. He could joke easily with someone he had just met, and even take a slight jest at his own expense, but when a visitor let his guard down and went too far, Che's expression would turn icy. He often reminded his subordinates not to try his patience.

Che liked working more than anything else, but did enjoy his family during the few hours he allotted them.

He loved to stretch out on the floor with his children and play with them and their pet German shepherd. He never tried to distance his Cuban family from the child he had conceived with Hilda Gadea. Hildita frequently visited the Guevara home on weekends, and Che would watch boxing matches with his eldest daughter and take her to soccer games. Someday he would take on one of his foreign trips, he told her.

Che most wanted to return to Argentina as an armed guerrilla. In April 1963, his mother had been arrested when she returned to Argentina from Cuba, ostensibly for carrying Communist literature but more likely because of her famous son. She spent a few months in jail before being released.

Che finally came up with a way he could get a revolution started in Argentina without involving the Cuban government. The opportunity came when Jorge Masetti, an Argentine journalist who had interviewed Che in his guerrilla days, decided to become a guerrilla himself. Masetti set about organizing a rebel force in southern Bolivia. Che planned to join him in late 1964 or early 1965. In the meantime he would stay behind the scenes. He did not want his fame to draw too much attention to the rebels too early. They needed to set their bases up quietly.

Che most feared his presence would attract U.S. intervention. "The Yankees will intervene . . . because the struggle in Latin America is decisive," Che wrote in an article not published until after his death. "They will intervene with all of their resources and also will turn all their available destructive weapons upon the popular forces."

In fact, the U.S. had turned its attention to Argentina but not to the extent Che thought. CIA agents were on the scene, as they always were during unstable times in any Latin American country. But Masetti's problems as a guerrilla leader resulted from his lack of experience, squabbles among the guerrillas, and the lack of support from Argentinian people, not from the CIA.

Masetti's soldiers moved out of Bolivia in the summer of 1963 and hacked their way with machetes through the jungle to reach Argentina. They wanted to reach the city of Oran, where they planned to base their operations. But they instead ended up on a remote line of cliffs and had to retrace their steps. Lack of familiarity with the terrain cost them valuable time.

They also misjudged the political situation. The military leaders who had toppled President Frondizi organized an election and ran a right-wing general as their own candidate. Masetti's group naturally thought the junta leaders would rig the election to insure their man won. But voters instead elected Dr. Arturo Illia, a doctor from Córdoba known for his moderate views. When the military let Illia's election stand without challenge, Masetti decided his mission was hopeless. A socialist rebellion would need civic unrest to succeed, a condition unlikely to emerge after a successful election.

Masetti later changed his mind and wrote a letter to Illia claiming the election was fraudulent and urging him to step down. When Illia declined, Masetti traveled all over the country trying to drum up popular support for his rebels, but little was forthcoming. Masetti's nerves began to unravel and his men became sick in the jungle. Masetti had some of his own soldiers shot for laziness, and Argentinian authorities captured and executed others. Early in 1964, Masetti vanished, never to be heard from again.

One can only imagine the disappointment Che felt at the failure of revolution in his homeland. The failure left him dejected. He continued his travels as a diplomat for Cuba, but he was now more focused on finding countries receptive to his theories of revolution than in diplomacy.

Che had never physically taken part in the failed revolt in Argentina. He remained confident that all he would need was a small band of rebels to make another socialist rebellion succeed.

In 1964, a social upheaval in the Congo of Africa suddenly seemed to be a violent opportunity. The trouble had begun in 1960, when Belgium granted independence to its former colony. Belgium tried to retain its influence, however, and became one of several factions involved in a scramble for power in the Congo. American companies mined the mineral-rich land, the Soviet Union saw the opportunity to gain a Communist foothold in Africa, the Congolese military wanted greater power and influence, and the United Nations interceded to restore order. Anyone who tried to lead faced a whirlpool of

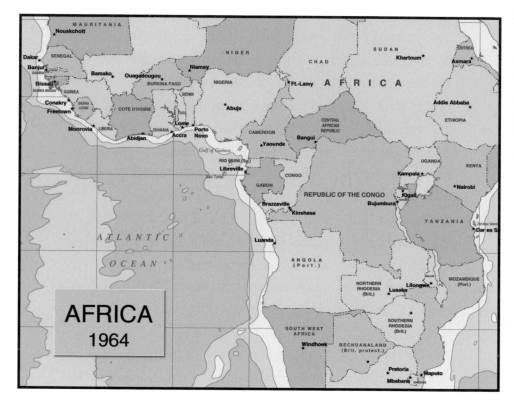

When Che traveled to the Congo in the 1960s, many countries in Africa were undergoing independence movements as they shed colonial control.

danger. Patrice Lumumba was elected prime minister in the country's first election and Joseph Kasavubu was elected president, but the new government faced immediate challenges from enemies within and outside the Congo.

Moise Tshombe, head of the copper-rich province of Katanga, tried to secede. Lumumba asked the Soviet Union for aid, which quickly got him labeled a Communist in the U.S. Since Lumumba was among the first native leaders in a land that had long been controlled by

Patrice Lumumba was the first prime minister of the Democratic Republic of the Congo when it declared its independence in June 1960. Forced out of office during a political crisis in September, he was assassinated in January 1961. (AP Photo)

European powers, Castro and Che considered him a natural candidate to become a comrade in arms in the worldwide Communist movement. But Lumumba did not live long enough to prove a useful ally. The CIA targeted him for assassination, but Lumumba had so many enemies its agents never got the chance. President Colonel Kasavubu conspired with army commander Joseph-Désire Mobutu to lead a coup against Lumumba, who was later executed. Cuba declared three days of official mourning to honor his death.

A civil war broke out in the Congo. Rebels who had been loyal to Lumumba set up a base in the town of

Stanleyville; the CIA established operations in the capital city of Leopoldville to provide weapons and planes to General Mobutu. Che watched the situation with interest as the war turned to a stalemate. The Belgians broke the impasse in November 1964, parachuting into Stanleyville in U.S.-supplied planes. They drove the guerrillas out, killing them by the hundreds. Backed by Belgian and American interests, Mobutu would become president in 1965.

Che was incensed and compared the Americans and Belgians to Adolf Hitler in their aggression against a sovereign country. He was due to speak to the United Nations the following month and used the opportunity to condemn the U.S. for their alleged involvement in the massacre.

When he arrived in New York on December 11, Che looked like a guerrilla commandant about to take on a fresh mission. He had his beard and hair combed, uniform pressed, and boots polished to a high gloss. At the podium, he let off a verbal tirade at the assembled representatives in their Western-style suits and ties.

The massacre in the Congo, Che said, showed "how the rights of peoples can be flouted with absolute impunity and the most insolent cynicism. The direct cause of all this is the Congo's vast resources, which the imperialist nations wish to keep under their control." The United Nations had claimed its mission in Congo was humanitarian, but Che charged the Western nations with harboring "hyenas and jackals," saying they

An affable looking Che makes an appearance on Face the Nation *at CBS-TV studios in New York City during his trip to the United States in December 1964.* (AP Photo)

collectively acted like "a carnivorous animal on the helpless." He added a call to arms: "All free men throughout the world must make ready to avenge the Congo crime."

Che was personally ready to lead the charge. He continued his diplomatic travels for several more months before arriving back in Havana. Castro and Aleida met Che at the airport, a special reunion in more ways than one. While he was gone, Aleida had borne their fourth and final child, a son named Ernesto. But Castro stole any chances for an intimate reunion, insisting instead on taking to Che behind closed doors.

Some have speculated the two quarreled at the meeting, and that Castro was seeking a way to get Che out of the country so he could rule without the distraction of Che's flamboyant and outspoken style. Whatever the reason, Che emerged from the talk with Castro's blessing for a military expedition to the Congo. Che had already contacted some of the Congolese rebels and he spent the next few weeks organizing an expeditionary force of Cubans.

As he prepared, his thoughts frequently dwelled on his own death. He wrote a farewell letter to Castro with the understanding that it would later be made public. He wrote, "If I should die under other skies, my last thought will be for you, my last thought will be for this people." In the same letter, Che resigned his positions in the Cuban government and renounced his Cuban citizenship. He said he wanted to free Cuba from responsibility for any of his actions in the Congo.

During lunch with Aleida, he dropped another ominous hint. He asked their nanny Sofía about the fate of widows of soldiers killed in the Cuban Revolution. He wanted to know if they had remarried. Many had, Sofía replied. He turned to his wife. "In that case, this coffee you serve me, may you serve to another." It was his way of giving Aleida permission to remarry in case of his death.

What Che found in the Congo lent credence to his dark premonitions. He arrived in Tanzania in April of 1965 and, disguised as a businessman, made his way into the Congo. There he found a disorganized, undisciplined group of rebels. The Congo of 1965 was different than Cuba in 1958. Che failed to understand that many rebels considered their expulsion from Stanleyville by the Belgians to be the death knell for their rebellion. Some expected they would soon die; others hoped to strike deals with the enemy.

Che's attempt to impose discipline turned to a nightmare. These people might well have been brave soldiers in their defense of President Lumumba several years earlier, but their fighting spirit was gone. Che wanted to teach them the skills of guerrilla combat. Instead, they tried to teach him about magic.

An officer explained to Che that their greatest weapon was *dawa,* a magic potion that kept them safe from bullets. When he drank dawa, the officer explained, enemy bullets simply fell harmlessly from his body. He showed Che some bullets he insisted had been repelled. Che thought the man was joking with him at first, so he went along with the gag. To his disbelief, he eventually found that dawa was no joke, at least not to the Congolese Army.

Che waited for the arrival of Laurent Kabila, a Congolese leader who had promised his aid. But Kabila was slow in coming, and other commanders squabbled over rank, with no clear leader. Che could not get them to obey him. He tried to get them to simply go five kilometers to set up a training camp in the jungle, but they refused on the grounds that they would need orders from a commander who was away in Kigomo to carry out such a maneuver. He tried to get them to establish squads for training. They promised they would, but said he would have to put it in writing. He did so and never saw the document again.

"So the days passed," Che wrote in his diary. "Whenever the subject was raised again (and I did so with truly irritating persistence), they always came up with a new pretext."

The Congolese were less impressed with Che's fame than they were with his credentials as a doctor,

Che discusses guerrilla techniques with revolutionary soldiers in the Congo, 1965. (Courtesy of Getty Images.)

a profession highly valued in the area. The word got around quickly in surrounding villages. Soon Che spent most of his time treating malaria, tropical infections, and venereal disease.

The soldiers vexed Che in ways that would have gotten them shot if he had been in full command. They played with their weapons, accidentally discharging them while drunk, wounding themselves and their comrades. They drank an alcoholic corn-and-yucca brew called pombe. Once drunk, they got in fights and refused orders. Officers passed out in front of the men. Throughout all of this, Che could not muster them for a single battle.

Finally an officer arrived who was willing to fight. Laurent Mitoudidi agreed with Che on the need to move the camp further into the jungle, and he also set the place to engage the enemy. The Cubans and Congolese would attack at a town called Albertville. Che was relieved at finally getting the chance to fight, but on the heels of Mitoudidi's decision bad news came from Cuban reinforcements. Che's mother was in a hospital in Buenos Aires.

The news was really much worse. Celia had died of cancer on May 19, three days before Che knew she was sick. In her last letter to him, Celia encouraged Che to continue his efforts on behalf of socialism. "And this is not your mother speaking," she wrote. "It's an old woman who wants to see the whole world converted to socialism." She urged him to help other socialist leaders in other countries. "Yes, you'll always be a foreigner," she wrote. "That seems to be your permanent fate." She closed her letter with "a hug, a great big hug," an embrace Che could never return. While the rest of his family gathered for her funeral, Che's only presence was in a framed picture that sat on her coffin.

Che now carried the weight of his sorrow as he tried to revive what appeared to be a lost cause. Finding his troops as undisciplined as ever, and just as frequently drunk, Che was now the one forced to postpone the battle. He persuaded Mitoudidi to wait for a while, hoping to gain some semblance of control over the troops. Then Mitoudidi drowned in a boating accident. Mitoudidi swam for fifteen minutes, but rescue efforts were hampered because the Congolese were convinced that a magical force was repelling would-be rescuers. Soon after Mitoudidi's death, Kabila at last proved useful by sending a replacement for Mitoudidi. But the replacement wanted the camp moved to escape Mitoudidi's ghost.

Finally Kabila sent the long-awaited order to attack. He called for the rebels to attack the heavily guarded Fort Bendera. Che was to stay behind. Che urged Kabila to consider a more vulnerable target, but Kabila refused. Che dutifully prepared two hundred soldiers for the assault. The battle was a disaster. A third of the rebels turned and ran before the battle started. Four Cubans and an unknown number of Congolese fighters died, and a diary describing Cuban operations in the Congo was confiscated.

At the very time Che suffered his worst defeat, Castro made his last letter to the Cuban people public, in accordance with Che's wishes. He read the letter before a live audience, including Che's resignation from Castro's government and his absolving his adopted country from any responsibility for his actions. His mother's words had proved prophetic. He was a man without a country.

Che fought on for two more months in the Congo. The government, well aware that it had the upper hand, offered the rebels a deal. They would withdraw their soldiers from battle if all foreign fighters would do the same. The Congolese commanders pressured Che to agree. He insisted the struggle could still be turned around, but the native rebels did not agree. Some struck deals with the government on their own. November brought more defections and a letter from Castro, urging Che to accept it was a lost cause.

At last, Che gave up. He and his men, along with some of the Congolese, boarded a boat anchored outside a small village. No glory attended Che's departure, only a scene of regret and misery. The boat could not hold all the men who begged to be to taken. "There was not a trace of grandeur in this retreat, nor a gesture of rebellion," Che wrote later. After the triumph of the Cuban Revolution, Che had become an almost mythic guerrilla leader. As Che sailed away from Africa, he was for the first time a failed revolutionary.

TEN

DEATH IN THE JUNGLE

While extracting himself from the Congo disaster, Che showed a brief flash of the commander he had once been. On Lake Tanganika, a Congolese combat boat had approached the rebels' vessel. Although they were in no shape for a fight, Che ordered his men to mount seventy-five-millimeter recoilless rifles on the prow to fool the enemy into thinking they were well-armed and battle-ready. The Congolese let them pass.

Che's display of his trademark bravado put an ironic footnote at the end of an inglorious defeat. Che had physically changed during the ordeal. He had lost weight and suffered with both asthma and tropical diseases while in the Congo. At thirty-eight, he was well past the age when most soldiers want to risk their lives on battlefields. Yet Che was not ready for retirement. Even as he retreated he compulsively replayed his memories of the African defeat and analyzed his mistakes.

Che needed to recover, mentally and physically. He and his men rested, first at the Cuban embassy in Dar es Salaam (the capital of Tanzania), then at a safe house in Prague, Czechoslovakia. He wrote candidly about his misadventures, essentially putting himself on trial for the mission's collapse. At the root, he decided, was his own failure to understand the nature of the Congolese resistance and to fully appreciate the defeatism of the native soldiers, as well as his inability to learn the Swahili language quickly enough.

If Che was to "export revolution," it might be best to do so closer to home. Castro encouraged him to use his skills in another rebellion in the Americas. He had remained in contact with Che throughout his Congo campaign. Castro had his own reasons to keep Che active in the field. In January, he declared 1966 the "Year of Solidarity" with guerrilla struggles throughout the world. Cuba pledged alliance with any people seeking to overthrow capitalist governments. Castro may have also had other reasons. The split between the Soviet Union and China was now open and was at least as tense as that between the U.S. and the USSR. Castro needed Soviet aid as much as ever, and in Soviet eyes Che was too close to China.

Some who knew both men, and outside observers, wondered if Che would be more valuable to Castro dead than alive. Martyred revolutionaries often make wonderful propaganda tools.

Castro's reasoning will probably never be known, but the initiative for his final campaign belonged to Che, who longed for his next fight with burning intensity.

Che had never let go of his dream of planting a revolution in his homeland of Argentina. But he dared not go back into Argentina so soon after the failure of the badly bungled mission he had organized. He needed a country ripe for revolution that was close enough for the brushfire he lit there to spread into Argentina.

After examining political strife in several Latin American countries, Che settled on Bolivia. After the military had toppled the socialist-leaning Revolutionary Nationalist Movement (MNR) in 1964, the new president, René Barrientos, had invited foreign corporations back into the country and allied Bolivia closely with the United States, angering the Bolivian Communist Party.

Bolivia seemed to be the best place to spark the full-scale Latin American revolution Che wanted. He had initially thought it best he not return to Cuba in order to avoid being portrayed as a Cuban agent, but Castro persuaded him to return to raise troops. Castro contacted Mario Monje, secretary general of the Bolivian Communist Party, and arranged for them to cooperate with Che. Castro also set up a training camp and called in the best guerrilla soldiers available.

Che returned to Cuba in July of 1966, although no one would have recognized the man who arrived as the famed guerrilla commandant. He had to shed his fame,

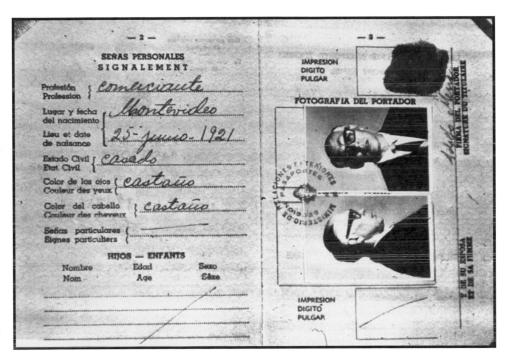

One of Che's fake passports, showing him bald and clean shaven. (AP Photo)

along with his identity, so he would not attract attention before his next bold military gamble. A barber had plucked Che's hair in a manner intended to resemble severe male pattern baldness, using tweezers in a painful procedure with very convincing results. He wore thick glasses and adopted a hunched posture, making himself look like a rather worn-down middle-aged businessman.

When he first addressed the troops who would accompany him, Che was introduced as "Ramón." He had some fun with his disguise, pretending to be disgusted at their lack of readiness for combat. As he continued his tirade, some of the guerrillas began to take offense. Who was this old bald guy to berate them as soldiers?

When Che revealed his true identity, they all had a good laugh.

It was one of the few times the band would laugh. The situation in Bolivia was extremely dangerous: a well-organized government army awaited them, as well as challenging terrain. Che worked the troops hard in training camp, determined not to repeat the mistakes of the Congo. Besides the physical regimen, he insisted the guerrillas learn the native language, Quechua. Once the revolution gained traction, Che also hoped to enlist the Soviets and Chinese for support.

A female guerrilla named Tamara Bunke, code-named "Tania," joined the band of recruits. She was a young woman of Argentine-German origin and had worked as an interpreter in Berlin, but had returned to Latin America to help work for worldwide communism. Che had met her in his diplomatic travels. Some gossip had linked the two romantically, but her subsequent actions would cast doubt on her loyalty to Che and to the revolution.

By the fall of 1966, the first of Che's guerrillas departed for Bolivia, where they set up a camp at Ñancahuazú. Before he left, Che had one last meal with his family. He did so disguised as "Uncle Ramón" to keep his mission secret, even to his children. He did not want them to know when they had last seen him, wary they might unwittingly tip off others.

His last sight of his children caused him more pain than he could express. Aleida played her role, introducing their father as their uncle. Only Hildita was left out;

Che feared his oldest child would see through his disguise. At the end of the meal, he asked the children to give him a kiss he could pass along to their father. Aliusha complied, and then loudly told her mother that the old man seemed to be "in love with me."

Che's disguise worked well in La Paz, where he passed himself off as "Adolfo González," a Uruguayan economist. From there he went onto the Ñancahuazú base, which he found well prepared. The rebels had disguised the base as a farm, with a brick house, a mud oven, crude wooden tables and chairs, and a radio transmitter.

But Che found other matters not so much to his liking. There was not enough foliage around the camp and no nearby peasant villages to begin building popular support. Only a handful of the guerrillas promised by the Bolivian Communist Party had arrived.

Che had other problems. Bolivian President Barrientos found out Che and his guerrillas were in the country and ordered the military to hunt them down. He had help from the CIA, which had managed to track Che's movements despite his attempts at disguise and which sent agents to help the president stop the insurgents. Barrientos also mounted a propaganda campaign, urging Bolivians to resist the rebels as foreign invaders. Bolivian soldiers courted the good will of poor farmers in the countryside, handing out antiguerrilla pamphlets along with school supplies.

Che contacted Mario Monje, the party secretary general who had originally promised his support to

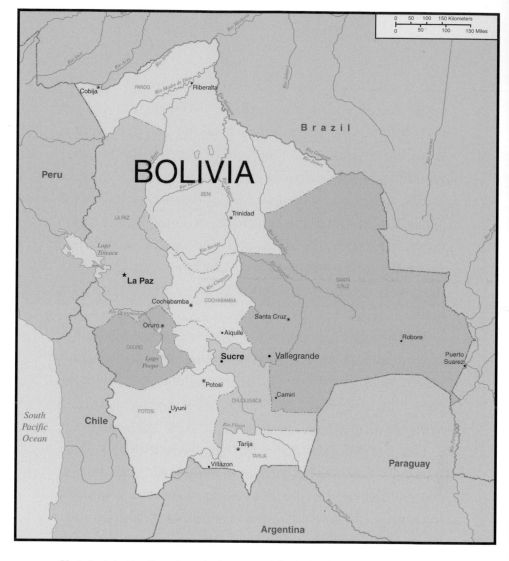

Che's last destination of revolutionary activity before his death. After he was killed, his body was transported to the town of Vallegrande, located in the south-central region of the country.

Castro. Che found his first meeting with the Bolivian Communist Party leader at the Ñancahuazú base bewildering. Monje's first question set off alarms. "Why are you here?" he asked.

Che thought Castro had prepared Monje for their arrival. Castro said both before and after the mission that Monje had offered support in full awareness of the guerrilla's intentions. Monje disputed this and claimed he had only offered to provide safe passage for the rebels to travel through Bolivia into Argentina. The truth may never be known. The controversy over the arrangements have led some to speculate that Che was set-up for failure and probable execution by Castro, who wanted to both rid himself of a potential rival and to concentrate on maintaining power in Cuba without Che's constant pressure to export the revolution to other countries. There was also increasing concern on his part about Che's apparent growing preference for the Chinese Communists over Castro's patrons in the Soviet Union.

Monje, an ambitious man, did offer Che a deal. He would resign from the party and bring in cadres of recruits for training if Che would agree to make Monje the revolution's leader and allow him to make all alliances with other Latin American leaders on his own terms. Che would also have to agree not to seek any alliance with the Chinese, because the Bolivian Communist Party was supported by the Soviet Union. Che refused. The best he would offer was to give Monje a leadership title in name only, a face-saving gesture.

"I'm already here and they'll only get me out over my dead body," Che said. Monje appeared to be swayed by Che's insistence and even promised to join as a soldier under his command. Then he left camp—and Che never saw him again. The next thing the rebels knew, Monje had informed members of his party that the guerrillas posed a grave danger and that they should either go underground or get out of the country. Che's band was now deserted, left alone to face the powerful Bolivian army.

Undeterred, Che set out to prepare the rebels for their first encounter with the Bolivian army. On February 1, he led what was intended to be a two-week training march. It turned into a forty-eight-day ordeal during which the guerrillas marched through a downpour, got lost in the jungle, and were reduced to eating monkeys, birds, and plants to stay alive. Even worse, two soldiers drowned in the overflowing rivers.

Back at the camp, two of the men deserted and alerted the Bolivian army to their whereabouts. Che sighted a government "spotter" plane searching for the rebel camp. He learned it had been circling for the past three days.

Under these circumstances, the guerrillas pulled off a surprising victory in their first battle. On March 3, they ambushed a column of infantry and killed seven Bolivian soldiers, took twenty-one prisoners, and seized a cache of weapons, including machine guns, carbines, and bazookas. Che interrogated the officers and later wrote "They talked like parrots."

The information provided during the interrogation of the two deserters raised alarms in both the Bolivia and the United States. Bolivia handed over all the information to the CIA. Dispatches about the rebels made it to the desk of President Lyndon Johnson. The reports stated that Che Guevara was suspected to be leading the rebels. U.S. advisors quickly trained the Bolivian Army's Second Ranger Battalion into a crack force of counter-insurgency fighters. The rebels soon were on the run, forced to abandon their camp and radio transmitter. Castro had planned to send reinforcements, but without any transmissions from the guerrillas, he did not know where to send them.

With U.S. forces on his trail, Che also had to protect two new men who were not soldiers. Argentinian journalist Ciro Bustos, along with Régis Debray, a Frenchman sent to relay messages between Che and Castro, joined the original guerrillas. Their presence added little to the rebels' advantage.

Despite the odds, the rebels pulled off several ambushes against the army, losing some of their own but inflicting greater casualties on the enemy. These successes against the odds might have been reminiscent of the Cuban Revolution, but the ragtag group did not have the strength to mount even a hit-and-run attack on any major garrisons. And without any Bolivians among their number, they seemed to be more adventuring foreigners than freedom fighters. The peasants offered them almost no support. Barrientos' attempt to earn the good will of Bolivians, as well as create fear of the rebels, worked. Some peasants tipped off the military about the guerrillas' whereabouts.

When the CIA raided their first camp, they found documents laying out the plans for the rebellion and photographs taken by "Tania" that identified almost every member of the guerrilla band. Some writers have speculated that Tania was a double agent who deliberately sabotaged the campaign. Her photos clearly helped the Second Ranger Battalion search for Che's soldiers. It is doubtful that Tania was a spy, however. She was later cut down by American bullets as she crossed a river.

Severe bouts of asthma, as well as depression, worsened Che's situation. Sometimes he was so sick the other soldiers had to carry him. His condition may have affected his judgment in April when he decided to divide his force in half. He hoped Bustos and Debray could rally support in the urban areas. There was also the chance that Debray could make contact with Cuba and ask for much-needed reinforcements. Both men, however, were quickly captured.

Che's beleaguered band walked into a trap in late August when they tried to cross the Rio Grande. They walked straight into an ambush that cost ten of them their lives. One of those who died was Tania. Twenty-three guerrilla soldiers escaped alive, but others were captured by the CIA, where they gave up valuable information.

Throughout September, Che led his decimated force through rivers and jungles, their chances of survival, much less victory, quickly fading. In early October, Che led his men into a canyon, which turned into a trap. The steep walls hemmed in the guerrilla force as Bolivian and American troops ranged the area in pursuit. Che proved to be wily, even on his last legs, evading the inevitable for days as fifteen-hundred soldiers dogged the fifteen remaining guerrillas.

The jaws of the trap finally closed on the morning of October 8 at the bottom of the Churo Gorge, when the guerrillas attempted to fight their way up the canyon walls against the Second Ranger Battalion. Che took a shot through the leg and another pierced his trademark beret. A soldier walked up to him with rifle pointed.

"Don't shoot," Che said. "I am Che Guevara and worth more alive to you than dead." The Bolivians took Che to a schoolhouse in the village of La Higuera and threw him roughly to the floor. Next to him were the corpses of two men already executed. Che could not have doubted what was to come. The execution order came down on the afternoon of October 8.

As Che lay bound, he could hear rounds of gunfire in the next room as his comrades preceded him to death. A soldier named Mario Terán was given the honor of killing the famous Che Guevara. Reports of Che's last words vary, but the most widely circulated have him defiant to his last breath. "I know you've come to kill me," he shouted. "Shoot, coward, for you are only going to kill a man!" Moments later, at age thirty-nine, Ernesto "Che" Guevara lay dead in the dust and gore.

After his death, Che's mystique grew. The Second Ranger Battalion strapped his body to a helicopter and flew it to Villegrande for photos and a public viewing. Hundreds of Bolivians and foreign observers filed past the body. It was as if the whole world had to be convinced he was dead. Shirtless, eyes open, with a peaceful expression on his face, Che looked like a saint to those who admired him. Much was made of his resemblance to classic paintings of Christ after the crucifixion.

This October 9, 1967 report from Walt Rostow, a top security advisor to Lyndon Johnson, advises the president that Guevara is likely dead at the hands of the Bolivian special forces the U.S. had "been training for some time." (National Archives)

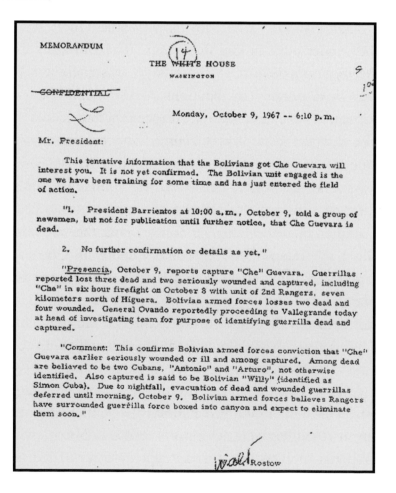

MEMORANDUM

THE WHITE HOUSE
WASHINGTON

~~CONFIDENTIAL~~

Monday, October 9, 1967 -- 6:10 p.m.

Mr. President:

    This tentative information that the Bolivians got Che Guevara will interest you. It is not yet confirmed. The Bolivian unit engaged is the one we have been training for some time and has just entered the field of action.

"1. President Barrientos at 10:00 a.m., October 9, told a group of newsmen, but not for publication until further notice, that Che Guevara is dead.

2. No further confirmation or details as yet."

"*Presencia*, October 9, reports capture "Che" Guevara. Guerrillas reported lost three dead and two seriously wounded and captured, including "Che" in six hour firefight on October 8 with unit of 2nd Rangers, seven kilometers north of Higuera. Bolivian armed forces losses two dead and four wounded. General Ovando reportedly proceeding to Vallegrande today at head of investigating team for purpose of identifying guerrilla dead and captured.

"Comment: This confirms Bolivian armed forces conviction that "Che" Guevara earlier seriously wounded or ill and among captured. Among dead are believed to be two Cubans, "Antonio" and "Arturo", not otherwise identified. Also captured is said to be Bolivian "Willy" (identified as Simon Cuba). Due to nightfall, evacuation of dead and wounded guerrillas deferred until morning, October 9. Bolivian armed forces believes Rangers have surrounded guerrilla force boxed into canyon and expect to eliminate them soon."

Walt Rostow

The Bolivians did not share that view. They only wanted to make sure the world understood what happened to those who tried to foment rebellion in their country. They had Che's hands amputated, made fingerprints, and distributed the evidence to the media as even more proof they had killed Che and not an imposter. They then buried him in a mass grave with the other guerrillas to keep Che's admirers from erecting a shrine. They claimed he had been cremated.

There his remains lay for three decades. In 1995, Jon Lee Anderson, author of *Che: A Revolutionary Life*, interviewed a Bolivian general who was present at the time of the execution. The general told Anderson what had happened to Che's body. Anderson wrote a story that appeared in the *New York Times* that pressured the Bolivian authorities to help locate the body. They found it two years later, and forensic experts confirmed that the skeleton with no hands was Che.

Che's body was taken to Santa Clara, the city where Che had helped win the decisive battle of the Cuban Revolution. His official funeral was attended by thousands as he was interred in an elaborate tomb. Castro addressed an emotional crowd, calling to mind the image of Che in death as he declared "his luminous gaze of a prophet has become a symbol for all the poor of this world."

Che's death, particularly at such a young age, helped to turn him into a cult figure among the youth of America, Europe, and especially Latin America. Some of the adulation directed at him surely would have surprised

Several thousand Cubans waited in line to get a glimpse of Che's remains while they were displayed at the Plaza of the Revolution in Havana in October 1997. (AP Photo/Joe Cavaretta)

the rebel leader. He died in an era symbolized by campus protests against the Vietnam War and racial injustice. The famous photograph by Alberto Korda was turned into a poster that decorated campus dorm walls with a romanticized image of one of the most famed revolutionaries of the day. The linkage between their causes and Che's were usually tenuous at best, but the image was more powerful than the logic.

Some of the young radicals in the United States no doubt confused how they viewed the word "revolution" with how Che Guevara understood the word. To campus protesters, it meant a change in society's values. To Che, it meant armed revolt aimed at bringing down governments. After the overthrow of Guatemalan President Jacobo Arbenz, who had allowed the media to criticize him, he railed furiously at Arbenz's tolerance of a free press. He never advocated free elections in Cuba, preferring the cult of personality that kept Castro in power. At a time when many protesters were antiwar, Che saw military force as the most powerful agent of social change.

Ironically, thousands of T-shirt vendors and others have turned the marketing of Che's image into a profitable enterprise. As usually happens with the establishment of posthumous cults, coincidence played a large part. The unkempt beard and long hair that Che grew mostly out of necessity during his military campaigns matched the youth style of the era. It also helped that he was darkly, romantically handsome.

Che's role in history may depend on how historians come to view Castro's rule in Cuba and his struggle against the United States. In Latin America, U.S. influence in the area continues to breed the same resentment that made such an impression on Che as a young man. Strong socialist movements still attract converts in Venezuela, Chile, Bolivia, Brazil, Uruguay, and elsewhere. Venezuelan President Hugo Chavez has recently attracted popular support by making speeches attacking the United States and has announced plans to redistribute wealth and land. In December of 2005, in the country where Che met his death, socialist candidate Evo Morales won the Bolivian presidency over a candidate who once worked for the U.S. State Department. Fidel Castro has remained in power through the terms of ten U.S. presidents, despite a decades-long embargo by the U.S. and several attempts to have him overthrown.

The Cold War between the Soviet Union and the U.S. ended in the late 1980s and early 1990s as the Communist government in Moscow and its client states in Eastern Europe collapsed. The USSR dissolved in 1991, and China has begun to blend totalitarian control with capitalist style, as well as rapid industrial and technological development. Mao Zedong would hardly recognize it. The end of the Cold War has left Castro weaker because it left him without his main benefactor. Che's legacy in Cuba may depend on who, and what, follows Castro.

It is not necessary to wait for the judgment of history, though, to know how Che understood his own life. He was always honest about what he believed and wanted to accomplish. Those who seek to understand Che will find a clear picture of him in the advice he gave his children in his last letter to them.

"Your father has been a man who acts as he thinks and you can be sure he has been faithful to his convictions," Che wrote. "Grow up to be good revolutionaries. Study hard so that you will have command of the technologies that permit the domination of nature. Remember that the Revolution is what matters and that each of us, alone, is worth nothing. Above all, always be capable of feeling deeply any injustice committed against anyone any where in the world." Whatever anyone thinks about Che, no one can doubt he lived his life faithful to the last message he left for his children.

TIMELINE

1928	Ernesto Guevara de la Serna is born in the Argentinian port city of Rosario.
1932	Family moves to Alta Gracia. They move twice again before Ernesto finishes school, to Córdoba (1943) and Buenos Aires (1947).
1948	Enrolls at the medical school at the University of Buenos Aires.
1950	Travels around northern Argentina on a motorized bicycle, the first of his "motorcycle" journeys.
1951	Travels with his friend Alberto Granado by motorized bicycle on a journey throughout South America; visits Miami briefly before flying back to Buenos Aires in 1952.
1953	Finishes studies for his medical degree; leaves for Bolivia, beginning another South American journey.
1954	Witnesses the CIA-backed overthrow of democratically elected President Jacobo Arbenz in Guatemala; escapes to Mexico where he meets Cuban exiles who participated in rebel Fidel Castro's attempt to overthrow dictator Fulgencio Batista; marries Hilda Gadea; daughter Hildita born.

1955	Meets Fidel Castro, who enlists him in a plan to invade Cuba; undergoes his first military training, specializing in guerrilla warfare. The Cubans dub their new comrade "Che," a nickname meaning "buddy."
1956	Castro and his troops set sail for Cuba on the *Granma*.
1956- 1958	Che distinguishes himself first as a soldier, then as a comandante in Castro's army.
1959	Batista resigns in January; Castro quickly takes power; Che presides over trials and executions of former Batista officials; marries Aleida March; becomes president of the National Bank of Cuba in November.
1961	Quits the job as bank president and is named minister of industry; the United States launches the failed Bay of Pigs invasion in April.
1962	The Cuban Missile Crisis grips the attention of the international community in October.
1963	Commissions failed Argentinian revolt.
1965	Travels to the Congo to help lead a nationalist liberation movement founded by the late Patrice Lumumba; returns to Cuba in December.
1966	Travels to Bolivia to lead his final revolutionary campaign.
1967	Captured by the Bolivian Army; executed on October 9 and buried in an unmarked grave.
1997	Remains are found and returned to Cuba; interred with full state honors.

SOURCES

CHAPTER ONE: Boy Soldier

p. 11, "For as long . . ." Robert E. Quirk, *Fidel Castro* (New York, London: W.W. Norton & Company, 1993), 584.

p. 14, "I would rather . . ." Daniel James, *Che Guevara* (New York: Stein and Day, 1969), 30.

p. 15, "There, nothing was . . ." Eric Luther with Ted Henken, M.A., *The Life and Work of Che Guevara* (Indianapolis, IN: Alpha Books, 2001), 5.

p. 18-19, "As a child . . ." James, 35.

p. 19, "He did not . . ." Luther, Henken, 9.

p. 27, "I initiated . . ." James, 37.

CHAPTER TWO: Threadbare Travelers

p. 37, "fills the senses . . ." Ernesto "Che" Guevara, *The Motorcycle Diaries: Notes on a Latin American Journey* (Melbourne, New York: Ocean Press, 2004), 34.

p. 37, "nasty, ill-tempered," Ibid., 53.

p. 37, "Two Argentine Leprosy . . ." Ibid., 59.

p. 38, "motorized bums" Ibid., 63.

p. 39, "The couple, numb . . ." Ibid., 79.

p. 39, "Whatever the outcome . . ." Ibid., 81.

CHAPTER THREE: Young Rebel

p. 41, "the lands and . . ." Luther, Henken, 30.

p. 41, "the sick of . . ." Ibid., 26.

p. 44, "The [MNR] is . . ." Ricardo Rojo, *My Friend Che* (New York: The Dial Press, Inc., 1968), 28.

p. 52, "I would not . . ." Paul J. Dosal, *Comandante Che: Guerrilla Soldier, Commander and Strategist, 1956-1967*

(University Park, PA: The Pennsylvania State University
Press, 2003), 34.
p. 54, "For me 'Che' . . ." James, 81.
p. 58, "He could have . . ." Dosal, 41.
p. 59, "I was born . . ." Ibid.

CHAPTER FOUR: Guerrillas in Training
p. 60, "The potential market . . ." Rojo, 60.
p. 64, "stop whining and . . ." Luther, Henken, 67.
p. 69, "Because he is . . ." Dosal, 63.
p. 72, "I wouldn't deceive . . ." Quirk, 119.

CHAPTER FIVE: A Dangerous Landing
p. 75, "We reached solid . . ." Jay Mallin, editor, *"Che" Guevara
on Revolution: A Documentary Overview* (Coral Gables, FL:
University of Miami Press, 1969), 52.
p. 77, "These were happy . . ." Ibid., 53.
p. 79, "have faith that . . ." Luther, Henken, 95.
p. 83, "Just then a . . ." Dosal, 83.

CHAPTER SIX: Triumph
p. 86-87, "Fidel Castro, the . . ." Quirk, 131-2.
p. 87, "a full account to the world . . ." Mallin, 54.
p. 90, "Put down Comandante." Ibid., 94.
p. 94, "with peace and . . ." Dosal, 109.
p. 99, "the Communists are . . ." Ibid., 151.
p. 99, "the passage from . . ." Dosal, 152.
p. 100, "dirty and skinny" Anderson, 356.
p. 101, "And from that . . ." Ibid., 361.
p. 103, "No, no, no . . ." Dosal, 159.

CHAPTER SEVEN: High Executioner
p. 110, "The most obvious . . ." Dosal, 165.

p. 111, "shone upon seeing . . ." Anderson, 386.

p. 117, "He answered me . . ." Ibid., 390.

p. 119, "The Revolution has . . ." Ibid., 393.

p. 121, "I feel not . . ." Luther, Henken, 130.

p. 123, "Is there an . . ." James, 117.

p. 123, "Fidel's crazy. Every . . ." Luther, Henken, 133.

p. 124, "For the [stuff] . . ." Anderson, 455.

CHAPTER EIGHT: Showdown with the U.S.

p. 126, "[B]ecause he has . . ." Tom Wicker, *One of Us: Richard Nixon and the American Dream* (New York: Random House, 1991), 157.

p. 129, "Although I had . . ." Anderson, 463.

p. 129, ". . . Che interrupted and . . ." Ibid.

p. 134, "Homeland or death!" Luther, Henken, 154.

p. 139, "politicians dressed up . . ." Roland E. Bonachea and Nelson P. Valdes, editors, *Che: The Selected Works of Ernesto Guevara* (Cambridge, MA: The MIT Press, 1969), 281.

p. 139-140, "Don't you get . . ." Ibid., 278.

p. 140, "guarantee that we . . ." Ibid., 295.

p. 141, "Anything that can . . ." Anderson, 527.

p. 142, "full retaliatory response," Quirk, 430.

CHAPTER NINE: Failed Rebellions

p. 151-152, "The Yankees will . . ." Bonachea, Valdes, 86.

p. 156, "how the rights . . ." Ibid., 337.

p. 156-157, "hyenas and jackals," Ibid., 339.

p. 158, "If I should . . ." Luther, Henken, 189.

p. 158, "In that case . . ." Anderson, 629.

p. 160, "So the days . . ." William Gálvez, *Che in Africa: Che Guevara's Congo Diary* (New York: Ocean Press, 1999), 69.

p. 161-162, "And this is . . . a great big hug." Rojo, 174-175.

p. 163, "There was not . . ." Henken, Luther, 202.

CHAPTER TEN: Death in the Jungle

p. 169, "in love with . . ." Anderson, 700.

p. 170, "Why are you . . ." Richard Harris, *Death of a Revolutionary: Che Guevara's Last Mission* (New York: W.W. Norton & Company, Inc., 1970), 152.

p. 171, "I'm already here . . ." Luther, Henken, 213.

p. 172, "They talked like . . ." Anderson, 710.

p. 175, "Don't shoot," Luther, Henken, 221.

p. 175, "I know you've . . ." Anderson, 739.

p. 177, "his luminous gaze . . ." Luther, Henken, 230.

p. 181, "Your father has . . ." Bonachea, Valdes, *Tricontinental Bulletin* (Havana, 1968), 36.

BIBLIOGRAPHY

Anderson, John Lee. *Che Guevara: A Revolutionary Life*. New York: Grove Press, 1997.

Bonachea, Rolando E. and Valdes, Nelson P. Guevara, Ernesto, 1928-1967. *Che: Selected Works of Ernesto Guevara*. Cambridge, MA: MIT Press, 1969.

Dosal, Paul J. *Comandante Che: Guerrilla Soldier, Commander and Strategist, 1956-1967*. University Park, PA: Pennsylvania State University Press, 2003.

Gálvez, William. *Che in Africa: Che Guevara's Congo Diary*. New York: Ocean Press, 1999.

James, Daniel. *Ché Guevara: A Biography*. New York: Stein and Day, 1969.

Luther, Eric. *The Life and Work of Che Guevara*. Indianapolis: Alpha, 2001.

Mallin, Jay, ed. *Che Guevara on Revolution: a Documentary Overview*. Coral Gables, FL: University of Miami Press, 1969.

Quirk, Robert E. *Fidel Castro*. New York: Norton, 1993.

Rojo, Ricardo. *My Friend Che*. New York: Dial Press, 1968.

Sauvage, Léo. *Che Guevara: The Failure of a Revolutionary*. Englewood Cliffs, NJ: Prentice-Hall, 1973.

WEB SITES

http://www.latinamericanstudies.org/cuban-revolution.htm
An in-depth review of Fidel Castro's revolution from 1952–
1958 as seen from both sides of the conflict. Features rebel
maps, correspondence, and images, as well as U.S. State
Department dispatches.

http://www.historyofcuba.com/
An extensive compilation of Cuban history from 1492 on,
including photographs and timelines.

http://www.marxists.org/archive/guevara/images.htm
Explores the history of the Marxist movement in Cuba and
throughout the world. Features many of Che's writings, rare
photographs, and a glimpse of his Marxist ideology.

INDEX

12/09   6   8/09